NAHANNI

PORTFOLIO SERIES

VOLUME 2

THE NAHANNI PORTFOLIO

Pat & Rosemarie Keough

INTRODUCTION BY NICK SIBBESTON

NORTHWEST TERRITORIES
CANADA

A STODDART / NAHANNI PRODUCTION

ACKNOWLEDGEMENTS

The Nahanni project was centred in one of Canada's most remote and rugged areas. Pat and Rosemarie Keough extend a very special note of thanks to the following Canadian sponsors, without whose dedication and logistical and technical support this book would not exist.

CANADIAN AIRLINES INTERNATIONAL LTD.
Two things come immediately to mind when we think of our warm association with Canadian and its employees: friendliness and efficiency. This large national carrier, with service spanning five continents, transported us and tons of our equipment to and from Yellowknife, the capital of the Northwest Territories. In our travels round the world, we have come to appreciate and rely upon Canadian's high and consistent standard of service.

NIKON CANADA INC.
We greatly enjoy creating images that capture the beauty of the natural world. Consequently, our equipment is often subjected to less-than-studio conditions. We have used, and abused, Nikon cameras and lenses on numerous journeys to remote and exotic corners of the Earth. From the humid tropics to the high arctic, rugged and dependable Nikon equipment has always come through for us. Our sincere appreciation to Hideo Fukuchi, Larry Frank, and Guenther Kresse.

NORTHWEST TERRITORIAL AIRWAYS LTD.
From Yellowknife to Fort Simpson, our jump-off point to the Nahanni Country, we depend on the friendly service of Northwest Territorial Airways. Through the years this pioneering airline has done much to remove the isolation of Canada's northern communities, to the benefit of residents and adventurers such as ourselves. Our special thanks to Northwest Territorial Airways staff, especially to Bob Engle, Jake Ootes, Peter Ingebrigtson, and Terry Denischuk.

GOV'T. OF THE NORTHWEST TERRITORIES
We are grateful to the helpful people of the Northwest Territories Government who assisted us in so many ways: aiding with administrative details, locating research materials, planning logistics, and providing warehousing and transportation. Our warmest thanks to Nick Sibbeston, John Sheehan, Terry Ward, Alan Vaughan, Bernadette Norwegian, Cindy Clegg, Bill Steward, Ethel Blondin-Townsend, Eleanor Bran, Christopher Stephens, Christopher Hanks, Janet Chatwood, and John Poirer.

PLATE 1   *The Upper South Nahanni River – July 1987*

OKANAGAN HELICOPTERS LTD.
This large Canadian company, with bases world-wide, has an unmatched reputation for high professional standards and safety. We feel privileged to have flown countless hours with Okanagan into the most rugged and inaccessible terrain in the Nahanni Country. Our sincere thanks to Jim Broadbent and Frank Carmichael – two of the finest mountain helicopter pilots in the world – and to Pat Aldous and Al Eustis at the headquarters in Richmond, B.C.

SIMPSON AIR (1981) LTD.
Ted Grant wears many hats: bush pilot, businessman, and politician. Ted's charter plane service flies from Fort Simpson, N.W.T., to many remote northern locations, including the Nahanni Country and his guest lodges at Great Bear and Little Doctor lakes. For all the flying, logistical support, tremendous hospitality, and so very much more, our heartfelt thanks to Ted & Noreen Grant and to Patty Gammon, Mansell Patterson, and Ron Sprang.

TRAILHEAD
Trailhead is much more than a quality retail outlet that specializes in wilderness travel, equipment, instruction, and outfitting. With stores located in Ottawa, Toronto, and Montreal, this organization represents much of what we believe in: respect for nature, wilderness adventure, and camaraderie shared among friends. We greatly value the help and advice of our outfitter and friend Wally Schaber. Our thanks as well to Wendy Grater and Jean Huard.

The authors express their appreciation to those, listed below, who have lent time and expertise to this book:

Kerry Abel, Michael Asch, Douglas & Susan Bassett, Robert & Birgit Bateman, John Cody, Derek Ford, Monte Hummel, Don Lafontaine, Henri Ouellet, Scott Redhead, Michael Runtz, George Scotter, and Wendell White.

The authors also gratefully acknowledge the following people for their unfailing support and co-operation:

Alan & Wanda Bowles, Steve Catto, Pete Cowie, Flora Czirfusz, Ken Davidge, Linda Davis, Jean-Pierre Gelinas, Wendy Groat, Angel Guerra, Bill Hanna, Arnold Hope, Jerry Irving, Mary Keough, Gus & Mary Kraus, Bill Lafferty, Peter & Beth Lamb, Sue & Edwin Lindburg, Anna Lindburg, Kevin & Kathy McCormick, Barney MacLaren, Ruth Montgomery, Mary Mortimer, Arnold Muirhead, Walter Murrmans, Andy Norwegian, Pat Olexin, Marigold Patterson, George Pellissey, John Robertson, Jeannie Sheehan, Karen Sibbeston, Jack Stoddart, Karen Tippet, Bella Trindell, and Vera Turner.

Gilles Couet – Chlorophylle haute technologie: Wilderness Clothing. Michael Mayzel – Daymen Photo Marketing Ltd: Lowe-Pro Camera Bags. David Bishop, Dennis Cannon, and Peter Scarth – Kodak Canada Inc.

Published in Canada by Stoddart Publishing Co. Limited
34 Lesmill Road, Don Mills, Ontario M3B 2T6

First Edition 1988

Canadian Cataloguing in Publication Data.

Keough, Pat, 1945-
    The Nahanni Portfolio

Bibliography: p. 177
Includes index.
ISBN 0-7737-2167-3

1. Natural History — Northwest Territories — Nahanni Region
    — Pictorial works.
2. Nahanni Region (N.W.T.) — Description and travel —
    Views.
3. Nahanni Region (N.W.T.) — History.
I. Keough, Rosemarie, 1959- II. Title.

FC4191.4.K46 1988   779'.3'097193   C88-093550-2
F1100.S6K46 1988

Printed and Bound in Japan

PLATE 2   *Lichen and Blueberry Leaves – September 1987*

PLATE 3   *The Ragged Range – July 1987*

*To our friends Bob and Birgit Bateman, who enrich
our lives and lift us onward through their belief,
encouragement, and continual inspiration and who do
so very much to help preserve the Natural World
in all its wondrous complexity.*

*I want you to see the hills in native profile,
along the shores of the midnight river.
I want you to see the noon moon bask above
the fields of the island flatland.
I want you to see the fury of the sunset
caught between white pillars of the high Nahanni peaks.*

*I want you to hear the rush of wind,
the whisper of legends and stories untold.
I want you to hear old trees moan, young fires
crackle, and ice tinkle in the spring.
I want you to hear the night through canvas walls.*

*I want you to know the ancient one, this land,
whose voice is likened to a thousand spirits chanting.*

Bernadette Norwegian
Artist and poet, 1955 -
Fort Simpson, Northwest Territories

CONTENTS

PLATE 5   *The Granitic Face of Mount Harrison Smith – July 1984*

INTRODUCTION

When I think of Pat and Rosemarie Keough, several images spring immediately to mind. The first one, and perhaps the dominant, is of two remarkably talented, energetic, and enthusiastic people. They make, quite simply, a great team.

I remember well a warm August evening when I joined Pat and Rosemarie for a climb to a ridge high in the Nahanni Range above Little Doctor Lake. By this time the Keoughs had been living out on the land for months, exploring the mountains, rivers, canyons, and plateaus. They seemed as fit and agile as the Dall sheep that live in these mountains.

We gained the summit. Without pausing to catch a breath, Pat and Rosemarie set up their tripod and camera gear. They began to photograph the lovely view of the setting sun and gathering storm clouds over the valley of the Tetcela River and the distant Ram Plateau. Far below, the sunlight was retreating up the mountain slopes. The deep waters of Little Doctor Lake were now inky-black. Up on our ridge, the lighting was rich and mellow. The shadows were long and accentuated. I sat on a rock to rest and enjoy the view.

I watched my two companions as they photographed the evening mountains. Here was a couple who obviously enjoyed one another's company. In their movements and in their communication, I detected a harmony of purpose and a keen awareness of their surroundings, which I found invigorating.

They drew together what were to me random shapes and patterns, and created beautiful and cohesive images in the viewfinder. Each blade of grass, clump of moss, or passing shadow of a cloud assumed meaning and importance. From time to time, they asked me what I thought. When I looked through the camera at their picture I saw the world in a different way. The Keoughs helped me see a particular beauty and intricacy in Nature that I might have otherwise overlooked. This is their skill; this is what makes them artists.

As dusk settled over the Nahannis, Pat and Rosemarie finished their photography session. We stood together then, quietly absorbed in the solitude, the magnificence of our surroundings. To the east, beyond the Martin Hills out over the Great Slave Plains, that ancient orange orb, the full moon, was rising. In the distance we could see Sibbeston Lake, a silver shadow on the darkening landscape of the low country. This lake was named after a fine hunter and trapper, my grandfather George Sibbeston.

As we talked, I reminisced about George, my grandmother Embe, my uncle Ted Trindell, about the Dene people,[1] Indian medicine, mooseskin boats, and life on the land. Pat and Rosemarie wanted to know about the history, legends, and stories of the native people, my ancestors who made their home in this wild country from a time before memory. I see now, as I did then, another image, another side of the Keoughs, which I have come to respect. They share a genuine thirst for knowledge about the land and its people.

I first heard of the Nahanni Country on the knee of my grandmother Embe, a Slavey-Dene woman who was nearing a hundred years of age. She was a young girl when the first white traders and missionaries made their way into the North. Back then life on the land still prevailed. Living in the bush was not easy. For the most part, the people lived a hand-to-mouth existence – fishing, hunting, and trapping – to feed and clothe themselves. They were always on the move in search of food and game. Shelter, if any, was a stick tepee or lean-to covered with spruce boughs or moose hides. Life was hard but good. It had its rewards, including a self-reliant independence and sense of freedom that may never be again.

Grandmother told me of her mother, who lived when the Nahʔąą Indians occupied the Nahanni mountains and lorded it over the Slavey people of the lowland rivers and valleys. The Nahʔąą were feared, for they had weapons made of metals found in the mountains and the advantage of flint used to make fire. Each spring the Nahʔąą would swoop down from the mountains in their large mooseskin boats, raiding and pillaging Slavey camps along the rivers. These raids continued until the Slavey bands organized and warred with

11

the Nahʔą̀ą, eventually killing most of them. Today, there are only a few descendants of the Nahʔą̀ą, a single family living in Fort Liard.

My grandmother brought to life the fascinating world of Indian medicine and folklore. Just as the beliefs and practices of Christianity are so prevalent in our modern society, in her day the interwoven threads of philosophy, myth, legend, and Indian medicine played an integral role in the survival of the Dene people.

Ted Trindell, my uncle, was a man of vision and eloquence, a philosopher. Ted showed me the way of the Dene, how they lived off the land. He told me of their struggles and achievements. He taught me the importance of the land and how to survive in the bush. He taught me never to waste or destroy, to use only what I needed, and never to abuse wildlife. He taught me to respect knives, guns, axes, fire, and water, for each is essential to survival. Yet, in a moment of carelessness, each can kill you, too.

It was Ted, with his flat-bottom scow and kicker, who took me on my first journey up the South Nahanni River. Ted showed me where he and my uncle Fred Sibbeston had prospected for gold and silver on Prairie Creek many long years ago. I saw the cabin that my uncle Fred and grandfather George had built near the mouth of the Flat River in 1942. Up the Flat near the Caribou River was a larger cabin. Here, my grandfather and his whole family had wintered over, trapping lots of fur and living like kings on caribou and moose meat. On the spring flood they came downriver to trade their furs at the Hudson's Bay post at Fort Simpson. At a set of rapids in First Canyon on the South Nahanni River they had a near mishap. Today, these rapids are known as George's Riffle.

What I saw as a young man on that first journey with Ted – the powerful water, the great falls, and the deep canyons – made a lasting impression. I gained added respect and admiration for my ancestors who travelled these treacherous rivers in their frail mooseskin boats.

Since that first journey, I have been drawn away from the land in the pursuit of higher education and a career in law and politics. The desire to do something constructive to help my people spurred me on. I became a member of the Legislative Assembly, later, a minister, and eventually the Government Leader of the Northwest Territories Government. This life has been fulfilling; but I have missed that close, spiritual contact with the land.

Ted, George, and Embe are gone now, as are so many of the elders. I feel a deep sense of loss, a great vacuum. Gone with them, too, are many of the stories, the knowledge, and a link to the old way of life. Yet, their spirits live on, and the land remains.

Pat and Rosemarie Keough have spent over a year living in and exploring the wild Nahanni Country. Few people know it better. From time to time I would see them in Fort Simpson when they came out for supplies. With excitement they would tell me of all they had discovered and experienced. "Nick, you must come with us!" And so I joined them whenever possible. Together, we have watched a big bull moose splashing through the shallows of the Flat River. We have tasted wild mint growing in the waters of a hot spring. We have walked the high ridges of the Ram Plateau and months later skied through the silver beauty of a winter landscape. We have shared bannock by a camp-fire and swapped yarns around the glowing embers.

In a world where people sadly continue to desecrate our natural heritage, much of the trackless wilderness of northern Canada remains virtually untouched. Here is a last vestige, a last chance to conserve and do something right for both the land and the Dene.

In this magnificent book, Pat and Rosemarie Keough show us a uniquely beautiful and geologically complex corner of subarctic Canada. Their lovely images and evocative writing speak volumes about the need to preserve such wild places before it is forever too late. Wherever I may be, this book will remain for me a touchstone to the rugged beauty of the Nahanni Country, the land of my forefathers.

Nick Sibbeston
Fort Simpson, Northwest Territories

PLATE 6   *Evening, Homestead Near Fort Simpson – December 1987*

PLATE 7   *Horned Grebe on Nest – June 1987*

PREFACE

Majestic Mount Christie stands in the remote Selwyn Mountains, 63 degrees north of the Equator on the boundary between Canada's Yukon and Northwest Territories. Its eastern flank is notched by several glacier-carved valleys that have small, crystal-clear streams flowing out of them to the southeast.

We pause now, after ascending one of these valleys from our camp-site below. Although it is early summer, the weathered, lichen-covered rock upon which we rest is etched in a glistening white tracery of new snow from yesterday's storm. We feel a deep sense of well-being. Here, in the shadow of Mount Christie, we are far from civilization and all its trappings. When we speak we do so quietly, almost reverently. We do not wish to intrude where the only sounds are the soothing murmur of running water and the hushed, gentle sigh of the wind.

The air is fresh. The sky a deep, dark blue. There is no filtering haze, no dulling pollution. The clarity and intensity of the light confuses one's sense of scale, making distant peaks stand out, sharply defined. They seem almost close enough to touch.

Not far above us, in a saddle near the upper end of the valley, are the remains of a once magnificent snow cornice. It hangs out over a dark, fractured rock face like a great, curved scimitar, the broad point arching gracefully downward. The cornice had started to form with the onset of winter's first, slashing blizzards. Winds screaming over lofty crags continued to sculpt it throughout the long, crackling, cold, subarctic nights when temperatures sometimes fell to 50 and 60 degrees below zero. Hard-packed and burnished to the consistency of polished concrete, its chalk-white surface periodically reflected the cool, pale light of the rising moon and the splendour of star-filled heavens ablaze with a dancing kaleidoscope of Northern Lights.

Now, caressed by freshening breezes and warming summer sunlight, the cornice is slowly melting away. The cliff below shines with slender, serpentine slivers where water plaits downward; the dull rock is enlivened by the silver sparkle. On the outermost curled lip of snow, jewel-like droplets of water form, to hang momentarily suspended like delicate, crystalline pendants. We watch as they fall, shimmering, drop by icy drop to the talus below. In small rivulets they work their way through the rocks, gurgling along down the slope. Soon the rivulets join together, forming the small, tumbling stream, barely a hand wide, that passes at our feet. Alternately disappearing and reappearing almost playfully, the stream bounces among the boulders in apparent haste to get down the valley.

We marvel that this insignificant little stream, flowing from an unnamed notch in the Selwyn Mountains, is the very beginning, the headwaters of one of the world's fabulous wild rivers: the legendary South Nahanni.

Our stream is soon joined by others. Quickly building in volume and velocity, it hisses over gravel bars between banks that are adorned with the first purple blooms of the delicate Arctic Lupin. Within a few miles, twisting and turning through a series of short, tight meanders, it enters a broad, swampy, alpine valley. In spring and early summer the surrounding heights echo the thundering roar of great snow avalanches, which cascade down the precipitous north face of Mount Wilson, an imposing and truly magnificent peak that towers above this valley. Here, the marshy ground and small, shallow lakes that are dotted with mats of floating sedge act like a sponge to collect meltwater and rain. This is excellent summer habitat for moose and nesting birds and is aptly known by canoeists and other modern-day adventurers as the Moose Ponds. These ponds are the starting point for many an unforgettable canoe trip.

Leaving Mount Wilson and the Moose Ponds, the South Nahanni River flows southeast to drain a watershed of over 14,300 square miles. Dropping more than 3,250 feet in 340 miles, the river passes through a land long-shrouded in myth and mystery before it joins with the Liard, a major tributary of the mighty Mackenzie.

Long before the first white people came to the Nahanni Country, the land held a mystique all its own. A band of Indians known locally as the Nahʔąą were said to live in that rugged mountain region. The natives of the lowlands to the south and east considered these mountain Indians to be "the people over there far away ... the enemy ... in the land of the setting sun."[2] The Nahʔąą were regarded with fear and superstition. Stories of giants, evil spirits, and wild mountain men were part of the native lore.

Alexander R. McLeod made the earliest recorded expedition into the land of the elusive and mysterious Nahʔąą people in 1823. He was the Chief Trader of Fort of the Forks, a Hudson's Bay post soon to be renamed Fort Simpson. McLeod's objective was to establish communications and expand the fur trade into regions "hitherto unexplored."[3] Through the years, other white men seeking furs and gold followed him into the Nahanni Country. As one after another macabre incident occurred, certain aspects of the traditional native lore were assimilated and interwoven into the white consciousness and stories. The legends of the Nahanni grew as fast as the river rising in full flood.

Rumour had it that in this remote corner of Canada's subarctic wilderness there was a hidden, but cursed, tropical Shangri-La. Beyond the reach of winter's icy hand, one could find warm, lush valleys with giant ferns and palm trees and, for those foolish enough to venture near, sudden death.

In 1908, the headless skeletons of brothers Willie and Frank McLeod were found along the Nahanni River in what is now called Deadmen Valley. A few years later, the skeleton of Martin Jorgensen was found by the ruins of his burned-out cabin on the Flat River, where he was prospecting for gold. The bones of "Yukon" Fisher were discovered along Bennett Creek, and John O'Brien froze solid as a rock while kneeling beside his camp-fire on the Twisted Mountain. These happenings plus the disappearance of several other people under questionable circumstances all added fuel to the fire.

The Nahanni became fertile ground for storytellers and imaginative journalists alike. Lurid tales were told of lost mines and the bleached bones of headless prospectors in remote, mist-shrouded valleys, of hordes of glittering deadmen's gold guarded by a white chieftess and her savage tribe of mountain men. The Nahanni Country became a place of dread, where even brave men feared to go.

For centuries the native people hunted and fished in this land and made it their home. However, not until the late 1920s was the myth of the Nahanni partly dispelled, when adventurer R. M. Patterson and prospector Albert Faille did venture up the South Nahanni River and lived to tell of it. Faille once said, "I didn't find any gold and for sure there's no tropical valley in there."

In spite of this reality, the legends persist – and why not! For they are indeed great yarns to be told and retold by the flickering light of camp-fires. To this day they are perpetuated in the numerous names that have been applied to features of the Nahanni landscape: Broken Skull River, Deadmen Valley, Sunblood Mountain, Hell Roaring Creek, the Funeral Range, the Headless Range, Death Lake, the Vampire Peaks....

For those of us who journey to the Nahanni Country today, who follow the small, meandering stream out of the Selwyn Mountains, the reward is not gold but the land itself. It is a place where one can find revitalizing escape in the unforgettable experience of wilderness, of sights, sounds, and smells – a world apart from our modern, congested, frenetic environment. Here is staggering, natural beauty on a grand scale – a marvellous diversity of flora, fauna, and scenery, including landforms unique to the earth. Here are karst labyrinths and poljes, boiling whitewater rivers, azure alpine lakes surrounded by razor-sharp peaks, thundering waterfalls, broad wind-swept tundra plateaus, sheer canyon walls reaching thousands of feet towards the sky, caves and sinkholes, rock bridges and muskeg, hot springs and glaciers.... This is home to Moose, Mountain goats, Dall sheep, Woodland caribou, Grizzly bears, Bald Eagles, and to rare and endangered species that include Wood bison and nesting Trumpeter Swans. This is a wild land, uninhabited and untamed, where Nature reigns supreme and man travels on Her terms. But, for all of that, this is a fragile land, as is so much of our natural heritage that we humans have so callously abused and destroyed.

To this day the very nature of the country, the unproductivity of the land, the rugged, steep terrain, the turbulent, dangerous rivers, and the highly unstable and unpredictable weather have helped to keep the area relatively unscarred by the heavy tread of man. For the most part, the Nahanni Country remains a pristine wilderness. In a vanishing natural world, it survives in its primeval state, a legacy from that time before civilization.

PLATE 8   *Virginia Falls, South Nahanni River – July 1987*

PLATE 9   *Along the Shore, Cow Moose and Calf — June 1987*

THE
NAHANNI
COUNTRY

A Glimpse
of History

PLATE 10   *The Tlogotsho Plateau and Deadmen Valley – August 1987*

1

THE LAND

Numerous adjectives are used to describe the magnificent, wild region of Canada's Northwest Territories, colloquially known as the Nahanni Country. All are appropriate, yet at the same time somehow inadequate in painting a true picture of one of the world's most spectacular and diverse natural realms.

This remote and for the most part uninhabited land covers an area of roughly 28,300 square miles. It is equal in size to the province of New Brunswick and nearly as large as the state of Maine. The Nahanni Country is bounded to the east by the Liard River and to the south and west by the Yukon-Northwest Territories border. A hypothetical line projected from the headwaters of the South Nahanni River to the North Nahanni and Mackenzie rivers forms the northern boundary.

Mountains, plateaus, wild rivers, and canyons dominate the topography of this wilderness region. It contains some of the most rugged mountain terrain and one of the deepest river canyon systems on the Earth's surface. The Nahanni Country also displays one of the most remarkable limestone landscapes found anywhere in the world.

In recognition of the geological uniqueness of this naturally extravagant land and with the objective of preserving at least a small part, the federal government created the Nahanni National Park Reserve in 1972. A 1,840-square-mile section was set aside along the lower two-thirds of the South Nahanni and the lower half of the Flat River, one of its major tributaries.

A bronze plaque stands next to a cliff-top trail, not far from the foaming thunder of Virginia Falls, a mighty cataract on the South Nahanni River. This plaque states that in 1978 the Nahanni National Park Reserve was formally dedicated by the United Nations Educational, Scientific, and Cultural Organization (UNESCO) as a world heritage site – the first natural area on the planet to receive this official designation.

In part, the UNESCO proclamation reads: "Nahanni National Park ... contains outstanding examples of the major stages of the Earth's evolutionary history and of significant ongoing geological processes ... ."

These processes are indeed ongoing, as they continue to shape the land we see today. The land appears so permanent and unchanging, so solid and enduring. Yet, with the slow, plodding creep of the passing ages, even the mountains and high plateaus come and go. Rock and earth are constantly moving as swift-flowing waters tumble along, carrying silt and even boulders; as river banks are undercut, sending trees crashing into the water; as deep, subterranean pressures cause mountains to rise, relentlessly inch by inch; as glaciers of ice and stone grind their way down from the high peaks; as water drips in the silent darkness of innumerable caves; as earthquakes contort the land, sending entire mountain sides roaring into the valleys below; as spring ice-flows abrade the canyon walls; and as the fragile, terraced beauty of tufa mounds is built up minutely, year after year.

West of the silty Liard River, the rampart walls of the Nahanni and Liard ranges rise dramatically above the flat, low country of the Great Slave Plain. Marching in a solid line across the horizon, they are the outriders, the sentinels of the vast, jumbled mountain kingdom that lies beyond.

It has been our good fortune to live in and travel through these mountains for extended periods. We have felt the pulse of the land and have seen the process of change. We have been awed by the savagery, the beauty, and the complexity of it all.

On one occasion, we were hiking along an alpine tundra ridge high on the spectacular Ram Plateau. Far below, a silver thread, the Ram River, flowed on its journey to the North Nahanni River. Nearby, on some moist, finely patterned ground, we observed the sharply defined tracks of a large Dall sheep. The animal was following a game trail that led past a limestone outcrop at the edge of the precipitous canyon wall. On this outcrop we spotted a fossilized clump of coral decorated with a garland of bright orange and yellow lichen. We marvelled that this lofty plateau was once the bottom of a

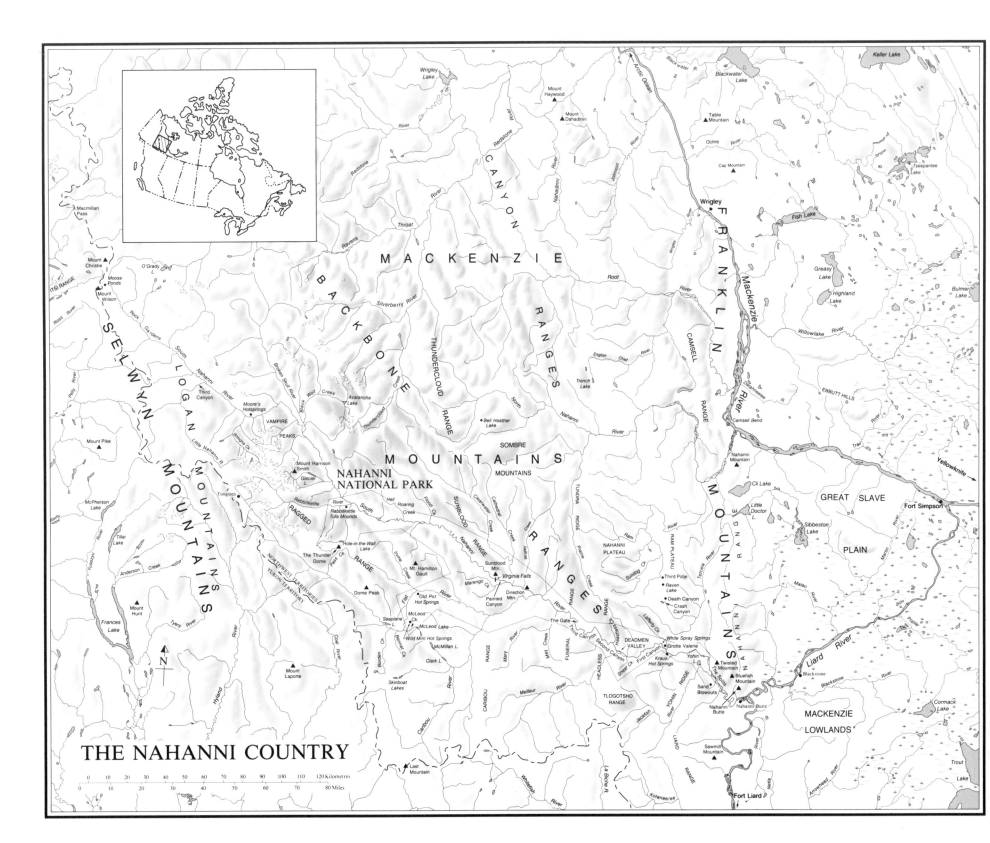

THE NAHANNI COUNTRY

warm, tropical sea. Here, written in stone and clay, was evidence of two distinctly different organisms at home in the same area but separated by the abyss of time.

The fossilized corals and striated walls of the great Nahanni and Ram canyons tell a fascinating story, a history of happenings in far-gone ages, before the mountains existed.[4]

Hundreds of millions of years ago, during the Precambrian Era, a wide trough had formed where the mountainous Nahanni Country is today. For at least half a billion years a vast, shallow, inland sea periodically occupied this depression. The warm waters of this ancient sea swarmed with a rich variety of marine life: algae, invertebrates, primitive fish, and extensive coral reefs. Successive layers of marine sediments, as well as sand, mud, and clay deposits from the surrounding highlands, settled to the sea floor. Eventually, these sediments attained a thickness of thousands of feet. Their great accumulated weight further depressed the Earth's crust into a geosyncline, an immense, bowed bed of sedimentary rock including limestone, sandstone, and shale. As these consolidated sediments sank, new layers settled above, thus ensuring that the sea remained consistently shallow.

On land the hot, tropical climate supported jungles of lush vegetation, which flourished amid steamy swamps and bogs. Through time, thick layers of plant matter were compressed into the Carboniferous coal beds of the Paleozoic Era. Coal from this period, some 300 million years ago, can be found in the Nahanni Country in such areas as the Tlogotsho Range. This indicates that at least part of the region was above sea level at that time, as it may have been early in the Mesozoic Era, the Age of Dinosaurs. For over 100 million years these terrible lizards walked the Earth, roaming the low-lying lands adjacent to the seas. However, in the Nahanni region, it was not long geologically before the sea flowed back into the trough. There it remained, acting as a great sedimentary catch-basin until the waters retreated for a final time. A vast, swampy, lowland plain emerged roughly 80 million years ago, as the long reign of the dinosaurs collapsed.

On the newly exposed plain, drainage patterns developed. The ancestral streams of today's South Nahanni, North Nahanni, and Ram rivers flowed from highlands rising in the west and meandered across the plain, depositing thick non-marine sediments.

About this time, as the North American continent drifted slowly westward, it began to override the floor of the Pacific Ocean. The friction and compression that followed caused the entire western edge of the continent to crumple and fold. The Earth's crust was uplifted in great thrust-fault blocks. This prodigious mountain-building activity progressed slowly from west to east. Eventually, it reached and cut across the ancient, geosynclinal sea-bed of the Nahanni Country. Large portions of this lowland plain were subjected to upfolding and thrusting on a colossal scale. Thus, some 60 million years ago, towards the beginning of the Cenozoic Era, the main ridges of the Mackenzie Mountains were formed.

West of the rising Mackenzie Mountains the associated movement of the Earth's crust had caused gigantic intrusions of molten magma. This upwelling lava was blocked from reaching the surface by a thick cap of overlying rock. Slowly, these immense, subsurface blisters cooled and solidified into granitic batholiths of grey quartz monzonite rock, thousands of feet thick. Over the ages, erosion and the sculpting action of glaciers exposed this tough, resistant, granitic rock, which forms the igneous core of the Selwyn Mountains. These mountains include the Ragged Range and the peaks near the headwaters of the South Nahanni and Flat rivers.

Uplifting and erosion continued during the Cenozoic Era, the most recent era of geologic time. Mountain relief increased, and the terrace-like surfaces of the plateaus began to take shape.

The area was crossed by streams, the dominant among them being the young South Nahanni, North Nahanni, and Ram rivers. These rivers maintained their meandering channels as they entrenched themselves into the rising limestone and dolomite ridges of the ancient sea-bed. "It was as though the rivers were great buckled knives and the ranges were slabs of butter pressed steadily upwards against them."[5] Canyons are normally carved straight and deep by swift, high-gradient rivers that cut downward. Here, where the land was rising up, something unusual was being formed – canyons that meandered in great, sweeping curves as they passed through the mountain ranges. Today, the canyons of the South Nahanni River extend nearly a mile below the surface of the Nahanni Plateau. These canyons and those of the Ram Plateau are the deepest and most extensive river canyons in Canada.

At the same time as the rivers were entrenching, a dense network of caves began to form in the Nahanni limestone of the rising plateaus. Ground water was channelled through these developing, subterranean conduits to a few springs along the rivers. As the land continued to rise, water sought new and lower routes to the deepening river channels. The old cave systems were abandoned. We can now explore some of these ancient caves, which have been left high and dry in the walls of the Nahanni canyons. Grotte Valerie in First Canyon and Igloo Cave in Death Canyon are good examples. White Spray Spring on the South Nahanni River and Bubbling Springs at the headwaters of Sundog Creek are the present and very active outlets of other underground rivers.

Thus, millions of years ago, the intricate features of the modern landscape, both above and below the Earth's surface, were beginning to unfold.

Concurrently, glaciation greatly influenced the emerging face of the Nahanni Country. For reasons yet unconfirmed, the world gradually slipped into the deep freeze of the Great Ice Age some two million years ago. In the northern reaches, ice-caps grew larger as winter snowfall outpaced the rate of summer melting. Under the impetus of its own massive weight, the ice spread outward. Continental ice-sheets repeatedly inundated Canada and then retreated during long, warm, interglacial intervals. Each of these advances involved two major glacier systems. The Laurentide, an immense flat ice-sheet, flowed south and west from Baffin Island and the Ungava Peninsula. The second sheet was the Cordilleran, a complex of smaller glaciers, which flowed east out of the western mountains where they submerged the valleys, plateaus, and all but the highest peaks. There were at least four major advances of these glacier systems. The Wisconsin Ice Age, beginning 25,000 years ago and ending only 10,000 years ago, was the last.

The complicated pattern of glaciation in the mountains of the Nahanni Country remains uncertain. There is no doubt that the region was heavily glaciated one or more times. Deep, V-shaped valleys, which had been carved by the entrenching rivers over millions of years, were scoured by the ice into the familiar U-shaped profiles that can be seen today along the upper South Nahanni, North Nahanni, and Flat rivers.

Early glaciation stripped the high plateaus of much of their overlying mantle of shales. The underlying Nahanni limestone, laid down so long ago by the ancient Paleozoic seas, was then exposed. The stage was set for the development of one of the most remarkable limestone landscapes found anywhere in the world. This is the Nahanni Karst Belt, a unique assemblage of spectacular solutional landforms, which were created through the ages by the persistent dissolving action of rainwater falling onto and percolating through limestone. It contains one of the largest natural rock labyrinths on Earth, where patterns of solutional streets and squares intersect. In addition, there are rock bridges, isolated rock towers, and numerous sinkholes and deep pits that lead to caverns and caves.

Certain areas, such as the Nahanni Karst Belt and the canyons of the South Nahanni, North Nahanni, and Ram rivers, escaped recent Wisconsin glaciation, and some of the earlier glaciations as well. These areas were spared the destructive impact of glaciation because, although the climate was cold, the advancing glaciers were starved. These regions were arid and lacked sufficient precipitation to build and sustain glaciers. As a result, the landforms that survive are among the oldest and best preserved in Canada.

What then of the Cordilleran and Laurentide ice-sheets of the Wisconsin Ice Age that assaulted the Nahanni region from the west and from the east?

In the Ragged Range to the west, many small but powerfully erosive Cordilleran glaciers grew. These sculpted soaring Matterhorn peaks, razor-sharp ridges, amphitheatre-like cirques, and towering cliffs. Today, when we stand in a high mountain meadow, surrounded by the needle-like Vampire Peaks, it is easy to comprehend why this alpine scenery is one of the finest and most rugged on Earth.

Out on the Mackenzie Lowlands to the east, the Wisconsin and earlier Laurentide ice-sheets had expanded across the Great Slave Plain. These glacial masses, starved of precipitation, encountered the barrier of the Nahanni Range. Although weakened, they had the power to breach these mountains, punching narrow gaps through the rock wall at several points, such as Camsell Bend and Cli and Little Doctor lakes, and a major rift at Twisted Mountain where the

South Nahanni River now leaves the mountains. However, the Laurentide ice advanced little further. With the climate warming, some 10,000 years ago, the glaciers retreated for a final time, leaving the low country mantled in a thick blanket of glacial till.

This extensively forested southeast corner of the Nahanni Country is now a landscape of gently rolling moraine and poorly drained muskeg that is dotted with numerous small, shallow lakes and ponds. Through this land flow the silty Mackenzie and Liard rivers. At their confluence near Fort Simpson, the Mackenzie is over a mile wide and is flowing swiftly to the Arctic Ocean. This powerful river is the longest in Canada, tenth longest in the world.

Laurentide glaciation had other indirect effects on the region. As the ice flowed through the newly created gaps in the Nahanni Range, it filled them. This formed dams, which effectively impounded the waters of the South Nahanni, North Nahanni, and Ram rivers. As a result, cold, freshwater lakes, some as deep as a thousand feet, were created within the canyons and mountain valleys.

These glacial lakes led to yet another anomaly of the Nahanni Country. The South Nahanni is a major river, comparable in discharge to the Colorado River in the Grand Canyon. As with the Colorado, one would reasonably expect a turbulent, whitewater river. Whereas the upper South Nahanni is indeed a thrilling, boulder-choked, whitewater run, the lower river descends smoothly with steady low gradients and only a few minor riffles. The true bedrock river channel, with its expected ledges, rapids, and falls, lies deeply buried beneath glacial lake silts of unknown depth. Today's river flows over the old bed of glacial Lake Nahanni.

Lake Nahanni sediments also completely entombed the original Virginia Falls. They now lie buried beneath the forest floor near the portage trail south of the spectacular cataract we see today. When the lake drained away, the South Nahanni River entrenched a new course that intersected and cut into the north wall of the old gorge below the original falls. Waterfall recession at an estimated rate of one-third of an inch per year has created the colourful gorge known as Five Mile or Painted Canyon. The present Virginia Falls is the largest, pristine waterfall of any consequence found in North America. The total drop of the falls and rapids immediately above is 385 feet – over twice that of Niagara Falls.

During the short 10,000 years since the glaciers retreated, Nature has shown its gentle side, slowly building and shaping fine features of great beauty, including the Rabbitkettle Tufa Mounds and the Sand Blowouts.

In the shadow of the Ragged Range on the edge of Rabbitkettle River, thermal springs well up through large, delicate mounds of coral-coloured tufa. These beautiful terraces of soft, crystalline rock are formed by the precipitation of calcium and magnesium carbonate carried in the warm spring water. The waters of this spring and others, such as Wild Mint and Old Pot up the Flat River, are heated at a great depth by the last vestige of batholithic-injection energy that created the Ragged Range. The lovely Rabbitkettle Tufa Mounds are the largest known in Canada and are quite possibly the largest in any subarctic or arctic locality.

The Sand Blowouts, tucked away on a forested mountain slope above The Splits of the South Nahanni River, is an intricate sandstone landscape that is more characteristic of a sea coast or semi-desert environment. Wind and rain have sculpted exotic, multi-hued arches, pillars, nubbins, and pedestals of all shapes and sizes. These fragile features had their beginnings in fine, soft sands laid down near the edge of an ancient Paleozoic sea.

Periodically, Nature shows another side that is sudden, savage, and destructive. A major earthquake in 1986, registering 7.8 on the Richter Scale, sent a cliff face plunging into the chasm of the North Nahanni River. Here, where time and a swift-flowing river have created awesome and tortuous canyons, the broken rock created a dam that temporarily submerged hellish rapids and chutes. Nearby, at Trench Lake, the same disturbance caused an entire mountain side, countless thousands of tons of rock, to slide away and roar into the valley below.

The land is changing, sometimes with infinite slowness, at other times with swift decisiveness. It is seldom still.

Today, the Nahanni region is a majestic mosaic of geological features, fashioned by Nature's selective hand. So many superlatives – the greatest, the largest, the longest, the deepest, the only – are correctly used to convey the extraordinary character of this land. The Nahanni Country, with its amazing contrast and variety, can be matched by few other places on Earth.

Nick Sibbeston and Alice Betsedia Tanning a Moose Hide

Charles Yohin, A Dene Elder

2

LIFE ON THE LAND

The camp-fire crackled and snapped as Nick Sibbeston added another stick of wood. He then stirred the embers, sending a shower of sparks into the black, star-filled night sky. Glancing up, he reflected, "If only you had been here 10 years earlier, you could have talked with some of the elders – to Charles Yohin, to my uncle Ted Trindell ... ." Rather wistfully we agreed. What stories they could have told us: the stories of their fathers, and fathers before them; the stories of the Dene people, who are part of this land and have lived here so long. How many fires have glowed in the folds of these mountain valleys – fires for cooking food and warming hands and hearts? How many stories have been told of times past, of a way of life that is now forever gone?

Commenting on these oral traditions not long before he died, Charles Yohin had said, "In the old times there were no books. There was only the people's word to go by. We listened to the elders."[6] Baptiste Cazon, another old and wise man, once said, "The old people used to tell us stories about how things are going, how to live properly, and how to live to be old. If you didn't live the way your dad told the stories, you wouldn't live long."[7]

Were it possible to trace the stories back through the ages, their trail would lead to Asia. Siberian hunters of the mammoth, bison, caribou, and other large animals that grazed on the Ice Age tundra entered North America by means of a land bridge that existed where the Bering Strait is today. The last migrants used this bridge some 10,000 to 14,000 years ago, shortly before it was submerged by rising sea levels as the Wisconsin glaciers melted. These people are believed by many anthropologists to be the ancestors of the Athapaskan Indians, a linguistic group that includes the Dene who are indigenous to the Nahanni Country.

The ingenuity, craftsmanship, and developing knowledge, which are integral to surviving in a harsh and unpredictable subarctic environment, was passed along by these ancestral people from generation to generation over thousands of years.

Through time, three distinct, regional bands of native people became established in the Nahanni Country. In the lowlands of the Great Slave Plain and along the shores of the Mackenzie and Liard rivers lived the Slavey. The mountainous country to the west was home for two bands of natives. The Mountain Indians inhabited most of this area. A small corner to the south was occupied by a group of Kaska Indians known to the Slavey as the Nahʔąą. The Nahʔąą were the mysterious Indians referred to as the *Nahanies* by the white fur traders of the early 1800s. The South Nahanni River was named after this group of natives.

Although they spoke different Athapaskan languages and are known to have raided each other, these peoples were affiliated culturally. They lived in a similar fashion, with some variation due to the geography of their respective territories.

Life on the land was a nomadic existence. In small family groups, the people travelled extensively over large, well-defined areas, hunting, fishing, and gathering what they needed. Virtually all of the land was inhabited, but populations were small. The environment, however, remained unaltered, for the Dene lived in harmony with nature.

This life was not an easy one. The annual cycle of activities was regulated by the changing seasons and the vagaries of the hunt. There were times of extreme privation, when each day was a struggle for sustenance and survival. Periodically, when game failed, people starved. But for all of that, life was good. As Nick Sibbeston says: "It had its rewards, including a self-reliant independence and sense of freedom that may never be again."

The staples of Slavey life were moose, caribou, beaver, hare, and fish, which gave the people food, fur, hides, and other materials used in a variety of ways. Snares made of sinew or thinly cut rawhide, called babiche, were depended upon for the capture of large and small animals. Bows and arrows, clubs, spears, and dead falls were also used. Fish were caught in nets made of the twisted, inner bark of willow and less often of babiche. Fishing hooks were fashioned from wood, antler, birds' claws, beaver ribs, and other bones. Hunting and fishing were primarily the tasks of men. Women,

Above: *Tepees on The Flats, Fort Simpson, 1924*
Below: *Baskets of Birch Bark and Woven Spruce Root*

Dene Family Boiling Birch Sap and Cooking Their Meal

children, and elders gathered roots and berries, including Wild Onions, Cow Parsnip, blueberries, and cranberries. Women were also responsible for preparing the food.

Food was commonly boiled in baskets made from birch bark or tightly plaited spruce root. Hooks of antler or wood were used to suspend these baskets from a tripod just high enough above a slow fire to prevent the baskets themselves from bursting into flames. At other times, in succession, red-hot rocks were placed in the baskets until the food was boiled. Sometimes meat was simply impaled on a stick and roasted next to the fire. In summer, surplus food was either dried in the sun on racks or smoked over a smudge fire and was then stored in raised caches reserved for the lean winter months.

Between other tasks, women tanned animal hides to be used for tepee covers and clothing. Moose and caribou skins, preferably of young animals, were scraped of flesh and hair. After washing and drying, the hides first were soaked in a mixture of decayed moose or caribou brains, urine, and water, followed by additional scraping, wringing, and drying. Then began the long and arduous task of working the hides to a supple softness, using a large stone or bone scraper. Later, over a smouldering fire, the hides were smoked for preservation and to give them a rich golden-brown colour. Only then were they ready to be cut with implements made of beaver teeth or birds' beaks and sewn into garments with sinew.

Shelters varied with the seasons. When travelling in summer, a lean-to of brush sufficed, or a simple tent formed by bending small trees over and covering them with moose hide. Tepees covered with hides or bark were used in summer camps. More substantial tepees banked with snow were often built in winter.

Bark from the birch tree was collected all year round, whereas the bark of spruce and poplar was gathered primarily in spring when the sap was running. Using a knife made from a sharpened caribou rib, the bark was peeled in large pieces, which were used for making baskets, tepee covers, and canoes.

In the North, where large birch trees are scarce, birch-bark canoes were a patchwork of heavily gummed pieces. Consequently, the construction of a birch-bark canoe took much time and effort. A less durable canoe fashioned in a day from a single sheet of spruce bark was favoured. The men made these canoes for immediate use

to traverse lakes and rivers and to gain access to remote hunting areas. With care, these canoes could last two months or more. The secret was to keep the bark from drying out.

During the summer, groups of people gathered in areas where game and fish were abundant. This was a time of festivities when gossip of the past winter was shared, gifts were exchanged, and feasting took place. This was a joyful occasion when everyone took part in dancing round a central fire to the sound of drums. There were guessing games and contests of strength and skill; there was gambling and storytelling. For the young people, there was the opportunity for courtship. And for those with physical ills, concerns for the future, or other problems, this was a convenient time to consult a medicine man or shaman.

The shaman possessed supernatural powers received from an animal or bird spirit, which could warn of danger and be called upon to aid in a crisis. The spirit would talk to the shaman either when he was asleep and dreaming or when he was in a trance induced by dancing and singing. The reputation and influence of the shaman depended upon how many people he had cured of sickness and how accurately he could predict forthcoming events.

The people of the alpine country, the Nahʔąą and Mountain Indians, lived similarly to the Slavey, although they experienced greater hardship in winter. Whereas the Slavey could generally rely upon catching fish and snaring hares in the lean months, the mountain people could not. In the mountains there are few large lakes that are good for ice fishing, and hares are uncommon. Winter snow made the hunt for large animals extremely difficult, and the possibility of starvation often loomed.

Dall sheep and Woodland caribou were the prime sources of food for the Nahʔąą and most Mountain Indians. The hunters would locate herds, then surround and drive them into long brush fences where the animals were caught in snares. Mountain Indians living in the more precipitous ranges where sheep are scarce hunted Mountain goat, using snares and bows and arrows. Nearly all the kills were made during summer months. Large quantities of meat were dried on racks in the sun and cached for winter use. The Nahʔąą and Mountain Indians tended to stay in the high country, moving from valley to valley and along the streams, seldom

Dene Women Scraping Flesh and Hair From Stretched Moose Hide

venturing into the lowlands. This remained the case up until and even after contact with Europeans. Eventually, the lure of iron knives, copper pots, and muzzle-loading rifles drew them on long journeys out of the mountains to trading posts along the Mackenzie, Liard, and Pelly rivers.

These trading trips led to the development of distinctive mooseskin boats by the Mountain Indians in the late 1800s. Modelled after the Hudson's Bay Company York boats, these craft were up to 60 feet in length. Five to ten untanned moose hides were sewn together with sinew and stretched over a frame of pliable spruce poles. Down the wild waters of the Keele, Ross, and South Nahanni rivers came the mountain people, with their dogs, meat, furs, and other goods, in these remarkable boats that slid across sand bars and over smooth-rounded rocks.

Before long, all the Dene of the Nahanni Country were within reach of the white man's trading posts. An aboriginal culture that had existed virtually unchanged for thousands of years was about to undergo profound change – and not necessarily for the better.

Above: *Mooseskin Boat Made of Spruce Poles and Eight Moose Hides*
Below: *Dene Woman Ice Fishing in Winter*

Dene Hunters Carrying Muzzle-loading Rifles and Powder Horns

A TIME OF TRANSITION

On June 29, 1789, three birch-bark canoes, a large North West Company canot du nord, and two smaller craft moved cautiously out from among the crumbling ice-flows on Great Slave Lake. They nosed into the mighty river that drains this lake to the west. Dehcho, the grand river, the natives called it. On board the larger canoe was Alexander Mackenzie, a young Scottish fur trader and explorer. He held high hopes that this river, which today bears his name, would lead through the western mountains to the distant Pacific Ocean.

However, several hundred miles downstream, the great river made a notable swing to the northwest along the wall of the Franklin Mountains. Here, at Camsell Bend, near the mouth of the North Nahanni River, Mackenzie had his first doubts about his ultimate destination. His fears were confirmed when, after ten additional days of hard paddling, his venturesome party arrived at the cold, ice-choked waters of the Arctic Ocean.

Mackenzie named the long route he had followed the River of Disappointment – a reflection of how he felt at the time. The homeward journey, lining and poling upstream against a powerful current, was a wearisome struggle. On the evening of August 13, they camped on a large, low-lying island at the confluence of the Mackenzie and Liard rivers. In the near future this island would be the site of an important trading post, Fort of the Forks, later to be known as Fort Simpson.

Although Mackenzie personally thought the expedition had been a failure, he was the first European to contact the native people who lived along the Mackenzie River and to note various aspects of their culture. His explorations provided the North West Company the opportunity for rapid expansion of trade operations into a vast new area that was rich in furs.

The close of the eighteenth century was a time of aggressive competition and bitter rivalry between the new North West Company, based in Montreal, and the older Hudson's Bay Company, of London, England. This rivalry was a catalyst for exploration and expansion in the northwest. Along the Mackenzie River, the North West Company established a number of trading posts, supported with trade goods transported from far-off Montreal by canoe along a tortuous and lengthy route.

These remote and isolated trading posts were all, more or less, alike: "A small cluster of log huts surrounded by [a palisade of stakes] situated in a clearing in the northern forest, usually at some strategic point or at a good fishing place on a river. All were on streams navigable for canoes because the rivers were the highways and only in the winter time was travel customary or even possible over land."[8]

The first post in the Nahanni Country was built in 1800 on the banks of the Mackenzie River at Camsell Bend by John Thompson. Initially, the native people, who from time immemorial hunted and fished for sustenance, had difficulty in comprehending the white man's seemingly insatiable desire for "meat with hair."[9] For his part, Thompson became progressively frustrated by the low volume of trade, a result, he thought, of Indians who "pass their whole lives doing nothing else but fishing."[10]

Operations were moved further upriver to the junction of the Mackenzie and Liard rivers in 1803. There, James Porter established Fort of the Forks, known simply as The Forks. The following year, a hardy and enterprising trader, Williard Ferdinand Wentzel, took charge of this new North West Company post. Wentzel lost little time in querying the Slavey Indians about the unknown mountainous country to the west. Encouraged by what he learned, a second post, Fort Liard, was founded roughly 200 miles up the Liard River and was managed by George Keith.

Wentzel recognized that the success and survival of these remote trading posts, and for that matter the very lives of company employees, depended upon the co-operation and support of the native people. Without the Dene, the company was impotent. The

Above: *Hudson's Bay Company Trading Post, Fort Simpson, 1852*
Below: *On the Shore of the Mackenzie River, Fort Simpson, 1892*

Tepees in Winter

native people helped the newcomers adapt to the often intimidating conditions of life in the cold, subarctic wilderness, far removed from the comforts of European settlements.

In these early days of the northern fur trade, isolated outposts were expected to be self-sufficient in terms of food and provisions. Wentzel hired natives to hunt and fish for the staff at The Forks. Periodically when game failed, the results, as Wentzel learned in the severe winter of 1810-1811, could be frightful and disastrous for natives and white men alike.

That particular winter, hares were at a low point in their cycle, and large game was uncommonly scarce. Ice on the rivers and lakes was over six feet thick, making fishing extremely difficult. The situation was so critical that by December the natives were reduced to gnawing the very clothing they wore. In the fort, at the onset of winter, Wentzel and his men lived on stores of tanned moose hides and parchment skins. By mid-January it became necessary to break into the bales of company furs. On April 30, 1811, Wentzel wrote: "We destroyed in order to keep ourselves alive upward of three hundred beaver skins besides a few lynx and otter skins." These measures helped but little. By this date, Wentzel was the only person remaining alive in the fort. "All my men are dead of starvation ... . My own position is yet precarious ... . I am quite alone at the Fort, not even an animal to keep me company."[11]

For the native people, food shortage was not the only hardship they endured. White man's diseases were already making inroads. Wentzel survived his ordeal and later recorded that the death of many natives had adversely affected the trade at The Forks. This gradual decline in trade, as well as concerns of native hostility following a massacre of the traders at Fort Liard and mismanagement on the part of the North West Company, led to the temporary abandonment of the region and the closure of The Forks in 1815.

Increasingly, the North West Company was becoming financially strapped, dependent as it was upon the long and difficult trade route of rivers, lakes, and portages that stretched from the Mackenzie River across the continent to distant Montreal. Inevitably, the North West Company could no longer compete with the Hudson's Bay Company, which monopolized the short, economical, and efficient route by way of Hudson Bay to England. In 1821, after years of

acrimonious and often bloody rivalry, the two opponents were united under the flag of the Hudson's Bay Company.

Immediately, the company set about reorganizing trade in the Mackenzie River region. Wentzel, who had just returned from the Franklin expedition to the Arctic Coast, was invited to join the 'Honourable Company.' In 1822 he received orders to re-establish trading operations at The Forks and to oversee developments at Fort Liard. Shortly thereafter, The Forks was renamed Fort Simpson in honour of George Simpson, the first Governor-in-Chief of the amalgamated company's Northern Department.

From Slavey Indians who provisioned Fort Simpson and from those who brought furs to trade, Wentzel had previously heard rumours about a mysterious group of Indians living in the mountains to the west. The Slavey held a respectful fear of this band that they knew as the Nahʔąą – "the people over there far away ... the enemy ... in the land of the setting sun."[12] There were stories of killings and raids. Wentzel made note of the existence of these people, to whom he referred as the *Nahanies* in his writings. It was Wentzel who named the wild mountain river, associated with these remote and as-yet-unseen natives, the Nahany River. Today, this river is called the South Nahanni.

The new governor, George Simpson, was particularly anxious to make contact with the *Nahanies* and other Kaska Indians. On January 2, 1823, he wrote to Alexander R. McLeod, Chief Trader at Fort Simpson, of his concern that the Mackenzie District was becoming generally depleted of fur: "[I]f we expect to make profits we must extend the Trade to Countries, hitherto unexplored."[13] Simpson ordered expeditions to be sent along the turbulent upper reaches of the Liard River and its tributaries. His objective was to secure direct trade with these natives to the west and thereby circumvent and eliminate the middleman system that was used to supply furs to Russian traders on the Pacific Coast.

A few months later, Alexander McLeod made what turned out to be an unsuccessful winter expedition into the Nahanni Country in search of the *Nahany* Indians. Alexander was the first of several McLeods to be linked with the exploration and legends of the Nahanni Country, and the first white person to venture into that unknown, mountainous region. He, in turn, directed his clerk,

Above: *Manning the Oars, Hudson's Bay Company York Boat, 1913*
Below: *Poling a York Boat Upriver*

another McLeod, John M., to continue the search as soon as the rivers were open. In June, John M. McLeod left the fort by canoe with his party of Canadian paddlers, a half-breed interpreter, and several Slavey hunters.

McLeod's party trekked for a month through the rugged mountain and plateau country southwest of the South Nahanni River before coming across fresh tracks of the elusive *Nahanies* in the vicinity of the Jackfish River and Yohin Ridge. From this mountain ridge they saw smoke in the distance and answered with a signal fire. "[B]oth parties approached each other very slowly, yelling, Singing and Dancing as they advanced, at 7 P.M. both partys joined unarmed, each holding a small piece of meat in their hand – shortly after a Dance was formed, which amusement continued for the remainder of the day."[14] The following morning, gifts that included a mirror, an axe, a small kettle, and an old gun were exchanged.

McLeod again rendezvoused with the *Nahanies* the next summer. He persuaded their leader, White Eyes, to return with him to Fort Simpson. There, through an interpreter, White Eyes told Wentzel and McLeod that he knew of other traders on the western coast, but, "We never could believe there were whites so near our Lands ... else we should long ere this have traded with them. If it had not been for an old Gun from you last summer, we should have starved to Death last Winter."[15] He also indicated that most of the *Nahany* people lived further to the west, inhabiting the country around the upper Liard River. He said that three winters had passed since his group had last travelled into that territory for a visit with them.

Post records show that these *Nahanies* became regular traders at Fort Simpson and eventually Fort Liard.

Explorations continued over the next decade in search of new fur country in the highlands to the west and safe transportation routes for the returning fur brigades. Many of these explorers made passing references to encounters with *Nahanies*.

In 1837 Robert Campbell travelled from Fort Simpson towards the headwaters of the Liard River in what is now the Yukon Territory. Campbell was exploring in the vicinity of present-day Watson Lake when he chanced to meet a "remarkable woman, the Chieftainess of the *Nahanies*."[16] Campbell wrote that she was a fine-looking, fair-skinned woman who commanded great authority over her people, then about 500 strong. Through time, stories of this woman were so embellished that she became the white chieftess of a savage tribe of wild mountain men, guarding hoards of deadmen's gold – the very fabric of Nahanni legend.

By this date, Fort Simpson, the administrative centre for the entire Mackenzie District, was one of the biggest supply depots of the Hudson's Bay Company. In addition to staff quarters, an office building, and a sales shop, the fort encompassed several warehouse buildings, a blacksmith shop, and boat-building facilities. All goods and supplies were costly because they were transported from England and required two or three years for delivery via sailing ships, canoes, and, by this time, York boats. Consequently, the importation of food was an expensive luxury. Aside from small quantities of flour, sugar, and tea, the forts, of necessity, continued to provide for themselves and shared what resources they had.

The relatively long growing season at Forts Simpson and Liard, combined with soils of rich river silt and deep, discontinuous permafrost, supported gardens that produced a great variety of vegetables and grains. Fort Simpson supplied agricultural produce to many of the other forts, while in return receiving much of its meat requirements. To aid with provisions, natives were encouraged to trade fish, meat, and animal fat; for example, ten hares, four moose tongues, or four ducks were equal in value to one beaver skin.

Generally, the Dene arrived at the forts in spring and fall to trade. Although some natives walked to the posts, most came by way of the rivers. Their spruce-bark canoes or mooseskin boats would be loaded with an assortment of furs, predominantly marten, muskrat, beaver, and lynx. Other furs and skins included bear, fox, mink, otter, wolf, wolverine, moose hides, caribou hides, and swan skins. Some groups, like the Mountain Indians, brought large quantities of dried meat – moose, caribou, and sheep – as well as animal bladders and stomachs full of fat for bartering.

Through this trade, European goods were substituted for and added to traditional Dene implements and materials. The natives were discriminating and were not flattered by useless presents. Once they determined what was beneficial to them, they demanded it. Guns, powder, ball, knives, axes, needles, kettles, woollen clothing, blankets, and beads were among the sought-after items.

Above: *Packing Bales of Fur, Average Load 200 Pounds*
Below: *Fort Simpson, 1901*

Above: *Trading Fur at the Post Store*
Below: *After the Goose Hunt, Small Steamboat at Fort Simpson*

The impact of the fur trade was far greater than simply the introduction of new technologies. Throughout the 1800s, methods of travel were changing, too, as contact with the white man's ways increased. The arrival of larger and stronger European dogs facilitated travel in the bush. Prior to 1850, small native dogs had been used primarily for hunting. With the exception of hunting parties, it was customary for women to bear the responsibility for transporting essential goods. Now, in winter, dog teams pulled toboggans, and in summer they carried the packs.

In order to accommodate trips to trading posts, the Dene gradually made adjustments to their age-old way of life, some groups more so than others.

The Mountain Indians living near the headwaters of the South Nahanni and Keele rivers developed a new cycle of annual activity. After the fall hunt, made easier with the use of guns, these natives wintered over in their traditional mountain territory. Toward spring they would build large mooseskin boats, designed along the lines of the York boat. On the spring flood they would descend these turbulent mountain rivers to forts in the lowlands for trade. Upon their arrival the mooseskin boats were dismantled and the hides traded along with their cargo of meat, fat, and furs. After a mid-summer sojourn of visiting and festivities at the fort, these people loaded their pack dogs. Then, carrying only essentials, they headed back on foot across the muskeg to the high country.

Over time, the Nahʔąą were no longer found in the lower mountain regions of the Nahanni Country. Fierce inter-tribal warfare, raids by lowland natives, and white man's diseases decimated the population. Eventually, the few survivors dispersed to forts on all sides of the mountains, where they intermarried with the local people. The Nahʔąą disappeared from all but memory and became themselves part of the Nahanni legend.

By the mid- to late-1800s, the pattern of Slavey life along the Mackenzie and Liard rivers was becoming increasingly sedentary as dependence on the trading posts grew. In winter, family groups trapped and hunted in the vicinity of small fish lakes. With the use of trap-lines, dogs for transportation, and provisions from the forts, it was no longer necessary to move about as much in search of food. In summer, as in early times, groups of people would gather in large encampments. Now, however, these gatherings took place at the trading posts rather than at major lakes. Some of these people were employed by the traders as interpreters, fort hunters, fishermen, and also as oarsmen on the York boats.

Seeking companionship and assistance, a number of the white traders took local native women as their wives. These women helped the white men survive and adapt to the exigencies of life in the North. Their offspring, the Northern Metis, were literally children of the fur trade.

The Hudson's Bay Company did not encourage settlement around the forts. The company wanted furs, not settlers. It was thought that trappers had to be free to roam the best fur country. The fur traders did, however, seek the loyalty of the natives to individual posts through the extension of credit.

As the forts grew in size and became more permanent, another group of Europeans arrived, also seeking the loyalty of the natives. On the evening of August 16, 1858, the people of Fort Simpson were gathered at the river's edge to greet the York boat brigade bringing supplies from Fort Chipewyan. The first clergymen to arrive in the Mackenzie district, Father H. Grollier O.M.I., representing the Catholic Church, and Rev. J. Hunter, of the Church of England, stepped ashore. They believed they had come to a pagan land, into "the wilds after those whom [Christ] calls His lost sheep ... ."[17] Charged with evangelic energy, these two men immediately set about establishing competing missions.

The early emissaries of these two churches were often openly bitter and critical of one another. Each professed to offer the only Truth and proceeded to rebaptize and remarry those who had been previously dealt with by the opposition. Understandably, the natives were confused. Stanley Isaiah, a Dene elder of Fort Simpson, once commented, "The Churches used to fight over people. The people didn't know what to do. They were mostly out in the bush. The ministers and priests were fighting against each other. Indians didn't look at religion that way. The Indians didn't say much about religion. It's the person himself that counts. Religion is the law of Nature. It is already there. It is not man made."[18]

The natives were actively urged to settle at the forts, "partly because it simplified teaching the Gospel, but largely because [the

Above: *Sisters of Charity, the Grey Nuns at Fort Simpson*
Below: *The Catholic Church at Fort Liard, 1892*

missionaries] believed these changes were part of the civilizing mission of the church."[19] Through time, schools, orphanages, and eventually hospitals were founded, many run by the Grey Nuns who first arrived in the Mackenzie District in 1867. The intentions of the missionary people were good. However, time has shown that their actions were often ill-conceived.

In a letter of 1876, Bishop Brandin expressed the unfortunate attitude prevalent in those early days, the sentiment that it was necessary for the natives to become more European in their ways. "In leaving our missions these children will have nothing left of being savage but their blood; they will have forgotten their natural language ... they will be humiliated when they are reminded of their origins."[20] Over the years, the impact of the churches upon native culture was as far-reaching as that of the fur traders. The consequences were often detrimental to the traditional Dene way of life.

Nothing affected the sensibilities of the missionaries at Fort Simpson more than the revelry and disorderly conduct associated with the arrival of the York boat crews. In June, when bales of furs were transported upriver, and in August, when the yearly supplies arrived from the south, Fort Simpson was host to a colourful mix of people. The great diversity of "races, colours, tongues, and religions,"[21] along with perceived "bigotry, avarice, lies, routs, drunkenness, fights, adulteries, and sessions of sorcery,"[22] caused the Catholic priests to dub Fort Simpson the Babylon of the North, Devil's Island, and Island of Sins.

There were "Scotchmen, Orkney Islanders, Norwegians, Englishmen, Metis of both Scotch and French descent, Dogrib and Hare Indians from northern points with a number of their families; there were Chipewyan, Yellowknife, and Cree Indians from the south; there were Slaves from Wrigley, Liard, and Providence ... . Of course, most Slaves from the Simpson [area] flocked to the Island on that occasion for business, social entertainment, and recreation."[23] Fort Simpson was indeed a lively place!

The York boat was manned by a Metis and Dene crew of at least eight to ten men. This versatile vessel was introduced into the fur trade by Hudson's Bay Company employees who had come from the Orkney Islands of northern Scotland. In the Mackenzie District around 1828, the York boat, which resembled the fishing craft of the

Orkneys, replaced the large birch-bark canoe of the voyageurs.

Constructed of hand-hewn planks, this craft was up to 42 feet in length and capable of carrying six tons of freight. This was twice the amount of cargo that could be carried by the same number of men in canoes. These boats were propelled either by long 16-foot oars or by great square sails when the wind was following. To travel upstream, the York boats were poled whenever possible. Otherwise, the crew walked along the river banks, tracking the boats with long tow lines. It was not unusual for men to lose their footing on the slippery, muddy banks and to be swept away in the swift current. Many men drowned in this fashion.

The conveyance of goods in the Mackenzie District was always an expensive proposition. The Hudson's Bay Company continually sought ways to reduce this cost.

On the morning of September 24, 1886, the company-built steamer, *Wrigley*, arrived at Fort Simpson. This event heralded a new and more efficient era of transportation on the waters of the Mackenzie River and marked the passing of the York boat brigades.

Many of the Metis who had manned the York boats settled at the forts. Some become trappers. Others were hired to maintain a steady supply of cordwood to fuel the steamer's boiler. A select few were employed as deckhands on the *Wrigley* itself. Johnny Berens, the son of a York boat steersman, helped build the *Wrigley* and worked his way up from chief cook to become one of the most respected steamboat pilots on the Mackenzie River.

The *Wrigley* removed some of the isolation of the remote trading posts along the great river, bringing the outside world a step closer. More white people came to this hinterland, carrying their expectations of civilization – their culture, religion, language, morals, values, and social structures. These influences continued to affect the Dene, a people in transition.

First, the white fur traders had come seeking their furs, then came the missionaries seeking their souls. Now, at the close of the nineteenth century, another invasion was about to begin.

Across the glacier-carved peaks of the western divide, along the tributaries of the Klondike River, roughened prospectors found large, gleaming nuggets of gold. The North became the focus of gold-hungry hordes, and would never be the same again.

Above: *The Steamer* Wrigley *Unloading Supplies at Fort Simpson*
Below: *The* Wrigley *Dragging a Moose up the Gangplank*

Travelling on the Liard River From Fort Simpson to the Klondike, 1898

4

THE LEGENDS GROW

On July 17, 1897, the old whaling vessel *Portland* steamed into Seattle Harbour from the North. On board were a dozen seasoned miners with combined fortunes that equalled over one ton of gold. Almost overnight the imagination of the world was inflamed with tales of the riches that were to be had at the mere dip of a pan, of Klondike gold lying scattered like seed on the ground or just beneath the surface. Soon Canada's northwest interior was dotted with thousands of gold-fevered and, for the most part, green prospectors with their pack animals and equipment.

Up until this date, only a few white trappers had found their way into the Mackenzie River area. But the trickle of newcomers swelled into a flood as news of the Klondike Gold Rush in the Yukon Territory spread. Hundreds of stampeders attempted to reach the gold fields by way of the Mackenzie Valley. They travelled down the great waterway in a rag-tag assortment of boats consisting of practically anything that would float. They left the Mackenzie River at various points along its course, headed west up turbulent tributaries, such as the Liard, Keele, Arctic Red, and Peel rivers. When winter's white grip tightened on the land, some men holed up in tents and cabins or in dens tunnelled into river banks. Others pushed on with dog teams and sleds through the bitter-cold wilderness.

Many of these obsessed individuals were ill-prepared for the incredible physical and psychological hardships experienced as they assaulted the continental divide. Dozens lost their lives in the Mackenzie and Richardson mountains, a sombre labyrinth of peaks, canyons, and rivers. The utter despair of one individual is expressed by his last words scribbled on a sign tacked to a tree: "Hell can't be worse than this trail. I'll chance it."[24] And with that he shot himself.

Only the hardy ones and the lucky ones made it through to Dawson where few found the gold of their dreams at the end of the rainbow. Others turned back in total frustration. Some remained in the Mackenzie Valley and continued to prospect and trap.

On the maps of this period, the South Nahanni River was indicated by an insignificant squiggle draining into the Liard from a blank spot marked Unexplored. A handful of gold seekers tried the South Nahanni River route, which they perceived as a shortcut to the Klondike.

Jack Stanier and Joe Bird were two such men. In 1898 a native guide accompanied them into the maze of The Splits, up through the lower canyons, around Virginia Falls, and to a point beyond Rabbitkettle Tufa Mounds. However, following an ominous dream, the guide insisted on turning back. Continuing alone, the two became the first known white men to reach the headwaters of the South Nahanni. At the Moose Ponds they found an Indian trail leading across the divide to the Ross River. They descended this stream to the Pelly River and thence on to the Yukon gold fields.

Other Klondikers who ventured into the mountainous interior of the Nahanni Country remain nameless. In later years, adventurers and prospectors, such as Bill Clark, Gus Kraus, and Raymond Patterson, found old log cabins – ruins they attributed to these forgotten men – mouldering away along the rivers and streams. When discussing those driven stampeders, Jack LaFlair, an independent fur trader for many years at Nahanni Butte, at one time remarked: "There's one of them buried down on Granger Creek, and the bank's been washing out near the grave. You can see his feet sticking out. This is all part of the Trail of '98."[25]

Although the odd white prospector or trapper wandered into the area, and although the Mountain Dene travelled these highlands, their ancestral home, the South Nahanni River region could have remained merely a name on the map for many years to come, were it not for the mysterious deaths of several prospectors who ventured into this wilderness at the beginning of the twentieth century. These deaths became interwoven with the existing native folklore, and thus myth became mixed with reality.

Long before the first white men arrived, the Nahʔąą, who had inhabited the rugged and inaccessible mountain regions of the Nahanni Country, were viewed with trepidation by the Dene people of the lowlands along the Liard and Mackenzie rivers. Stories were

Frank McLeod, Pre-1905

Willie McLeod, Pre-1905

told of primordial beings: giants endowed with magical powers, wild mountain men who stole women and children, and even some who ate other people. These were the forces of evil lurking in that unknown land of rock and peaks.

Fur traders first heard these stories from the native people and added to them. Through the telling, Robert Campbell's fair-skinned *Nahany* chieftess became a white queen of European descent, ruling a savage tribe of head-hunting mountain Indians. Sketchy facts concerning hot springs became tall tales of lush tropical valleys, where monkeys swung in palm trees that grew out of the permafrost, and where "mighty dinosaurs and monsters of a forgotten age still disported themselves in steaming pools girth with rich and luxuriant vegetation."[26]

As one after another macabre incident occurred in the early 1900s, the very word Nahanni became enshrouded with mystique, which has endured until very recent times. Today, even people who are unaware of the precise geographic location of the Nahanni Country, have heard the legends of Deadmen Valley: of lost gold mines, evil spirits, and headless prospectors.

With the initial euphoria of the Klondike Gold Rush waning, a number of disillusioned stampeders were attracted to the mountainous country and wild streams of the Northwest Territories. Attention was drawn to the South Nahanni and its tributaries when an Indian named Little Nahanni brought rich, gold-bearing quartz into Fort Liard around 1900. From then on, there were persistent rumours of placer gold up in the Nahanni Country. Over the decades to come, many men embarked on what was to prove a futile search, for little gold was ever found. The Metis brothers Frank and Willie McLeod were among the first. Because of the peculiar circumstances surrounding their subsequent deaths, the Nahanni region gained much of its notoriety.

There are as many versions of the McLeod saga as there are storytellers. After all these years it is difficult to decipher fact from fiction. One of the few certainties is that, in either 1907 or 1908, the skeletal remains of Willie and Frank McLeod were found on the gravel bank of the South Nahanni River by the mouth of Headless Creek in the strikingly beautiful area called Deadmen Valley. The rest of the story is conjecture. It is believed that a mishap befell them on their return journey from somewhere up the Flat River where they had been searching for gold.

Who first discovered the bodies is not clear. It may have been a party of prospectors including: Poole Field, an ex-Northwest Mounted Police officer; Big Charlie, a one-eyed Indian; and a Lafferty boy from Fort Simpson. It may have been another McLeod brother, Charlie, who was accompanied by the first patrol of the Royal Northwest Mounted Police into the Nahanni Country.

Some fanciful accounts tell of Willie and Frank being killed at the hands of fierce mountain Indians or evil spirits. Other stories tell of a third man, a will-o'-the-wisp partner named Weir, who may or may not have accompanied the brothers into the wilderness, where he murdered them for their gold and the secret of a fabulous mine. Some say Weir, or Ware, or Wilkinson, was later seen with a fortune in gold dust and nuggets at a saloon in Vancouver. Some say Charlie McLeod tracked Weir down near Edmonton and that Weir shot himself atop a burning haystack. Others say a third skeleton was found upriver from Deadmen Valley and that this certainly had to be the younger and less experienced Weir. As for the McLeods, their skeletons were found lying under a blanket or, as some narratives say, in their bed-rolls side by side. Sometimes one brother was lying face up while the other was face down with an arm outstretched, reaching for his gun. At other times, both were tied to a tree. In all the yarns, the McLeods are minus their heads.

What really happened to the McLeod brothers was undoubtedly less colourful than the dramatic tales that have been spun around their deaths. They were probably homeward-bound in early spring when their boat was sucked into a treacherous ice-jam, which often occurs below Second Canyon at the entrance to Deadmen Valley. Rumour has it that their make-shift canoe was found in a driftpile downstream near Dry Creek Canyon. They likely lost all their supplies and either starved or froze to death. Scavengers, such as wolverine and bear, may have been attracted by the odour of brains decaying in the skulls and may have made off with the heads.

No doubt, the incident of the McLeod brothers would have faded over time were it not for the succession of suspicious disappearances and deaths that followed.

A few years later, in 1915, Poole Field received a letter from his partner, Martin Jorgensen, saying he had made a rich strike in the Flat River area and that Field should join him. Searching for Jorgensen, Field came across the burned-out ruins of one of his cabins along the South Nahanni River near the mouth of the Flat. Field was later to report: "About fifty yards from the cabin ... I found an axe in the trail. I picked it up and just around behind the trees I found Martin's bones or what was left of them. His gun lay close by loaded and cocked. We never found his skull ... . We came to the conclusion that Martin had been shot by someone from the cabin just as he came around the spruce trees; that his cabin had then been robbed and set fire to afterwards."[27] Field was convinced that Jorgensen discovered the McLeods' lost mine and had been murdered for the secret.

Poole Field remained in the Nahanni area, prospecting and later setting up a trading post at Nahanni Butte, which he ran in competition with Jack LaFlair. Field became good friends with the Laffertys, a proud Metis family, and often headed up the South Nahanni with the Lafferty boys to trap for furs and search for gold. They would travel overland in the fall with their pack dogs, trap all winter, prospect, and return by canoe in late spring. On one of these trips homeward, Jonas Lafferty tipped his overloaded canoe, spilling his furs, dogs, and brother Jim into the freezing waters of the silty South Nahanni River. As Jonas was a fine canoeist who knew the river intimately and who later became the pilot of the *S.S. Distributor* on the Mackenzie River, Poole Field never let him forget this mistake. And so today, canoeists continue to be challenged by the little rapid known as Lafferty's Riffle, which lies on the South Nahanni just downstream from Lafferty Creek.

Along the Liard River Below the Nahanni Range, 1892

In 1921 Poole Field, his wife, Mary Adelle Lafferty, her cousin May, and a group of Dene were returning from the headwaters of the Meillure River where they had spent the winter trapping. One day May went missing, and she, too, was never seen again. Dick Turner, a colourful and knowledgeable resident of the Nahanni area, recounted this story that he heard from Field himself.

"Poole and the five good hunters – Diamond C, Boston Jack, Yohin, Tetso, and Big Charlie – followed May for nine days ... . She was wearing moccassins and her tracks were quite visible whenever she crossed a sand bar on the creek. But where she took to the bush there was little sign that she had passed that way. Once in a while Poole could see a definite footprint in the soft moss, and when they came to rocky or hard ground even the Indians would lose the track. They would circle around far ahead and always one would give a

call that he had found it again. To make it disconcerting for them all, the girl was apparently losing whatever marbles she had left. She would stop occasionally and divest herself of some article of clothing until Poole said she must have been stark naked. And with the mosquitoes so thick there was no way she could live for very long. ... About the fifth day the hunters came to the bottom of a very rugged high cliff, which was actually the side of a five thousand foot mountain. Her tracks were visible at the bottom but they could find no sign that she had turned to the left or the right. Poole said there was just no way that any sane person could possibly have gone up that wall of rock. ... Poole thought for sure they had come to the end of the trail, but they worked their way around to the top and sure enough, there was her track again heading south and east. Sane or not she was heading in the direction of her home, which was [Fort]

A Group of Dene Who Lived Along the Liard River

The Lafferty Family, Including Jonas in the Carriage, and Satone, the Dog, at Their Home on The Flats, Fort Simpson, 1903

Simpson. The search party was killing sheep and caribou for food and after nine days they only had six shells left among them. Just short of the canyons of Deadmen Valley they abandoned the search and turned back for Mary River."[28] May Creek, a tributary of Mary River, was named after the lost girl.

Not long afterwards, in the winter of 1921-1922, John O'Brien, a veteran of World War I, was trapping in the vicinity of the Twisted Mountain. Jonas Lafferty stopped by O'Brien's cabin and, not finding his friend, went searching for him. Atop the mountain at the end of his trap-line, Lafferty found O'Brien frozen solid as a rock, kneeling by the remains of his fire. The man's arms must been so cold that he couldn't even strike the matches that he clutched in his hands to relight the fire. For many years the Twisted Mountain with its distinctive shape was known as O'Brien's Mountain.

These stories, and so many more, helped reinforce the aura of mystery and evil that seemed to permeate the ruggedly beautiful Nahanni Country. There was Angus Hall who, impatient with the slow pace of his companions, marched on ahead over a ridge and was never seen again. The charred skeleton of Phil Powers was found amid the ashes of his cabin at the mouth of Irvine Creek. Partners Bill Epler and Joe Mulholland disappeared, leaving only their burned-out cabin near Glacier Lake. Over time these incidents, some explainable and other admittedly peculiar, became magnified and distorted. The legends grew.

Every few years the newspapers in the South would pick up on a rumoured gold strike in the Valley of Vanishing Men. The prospecting efforts of Poole Field and others like the Lafferty boys led to several minor rushes, such as those of 1922 and 1929, that

Poole Field (left) *With Companion and Pack Dogs Above Prairie Creek*

Fred McLeod, Brother of Frank and Willie, and Chief Dried Meat, Fort Liard, 1917

were publicized in typically dramatic fashion in the *Edmonton Journal*. "Land of terror and mystery, where the bones of slain prospectors have lain bleaching in the snow and sun for two decades, land haunted by horror and strange tales of witchcraft and torture, the Nahanni is to have the veil which has shrouded it for 25 years torn aside by the thousands who will stampede into the country this summer in search of gold which is said to be in the gravel of the creeks and rivers."[29] And so the stories continued. "You can kick the gravel heaps ... and see the gold gleaming like butter."[30]

For quite some time the Nahanni was billed as a second Klondike by a nation slipping towards the doldrum days of the depression years. No journalist ever stopped to ask why all these riches had been overlooked by previous parties. Needless to say, nothing much ever materialized, and no one found their El Dorado. But the optimism never really died. With its promise of gold, the Nahanni continued to lure more white men than it ever had in the past with its furs or souls.

Above: *Jack LaFlair's Trading Post, Nahanni Butte, 1927*
Below: *Gold Seekers Who Participated in the 1922 Nahanni Gold Rush*

Gus Kraus, Albert Faille, and Bill Clarke Sluicing for Gold on Bennett Creek, 1936

5

THE NEWCOMERS

The remote and relatively unexplored Nahanni region, with its rumours of gold, lost mines, and vanishing prospectors, was viewed as one of the last true frontiers by many men of independent bent. These restless individuals felt stifled by what they perceived as the encroaching encumbrances of so-called civilized society with its laws, regulations, and order. These men craved freedom, adventure, and the right to be left alone to make their own way in an uncrowded land where life was reduced to the basics and Nature was the principal adversary. By the mid-1920s few such places were left on the continent, or for that matter anywhere on Earth. However, in the Nahanni Country, amid the sculpted peaks and deep canyons, a man could still disappear for a year or more, and no one would think anything of it.

Many who journeyed to the Nahanni in search of gold and furs or to hunt for food are all but forgotten. A few others are well known and remembered for various reasons. The names of some of these men have become so closely associated with the Nahanni that they, too, are now part of the legend.

Albert Faille was one of these, a loner who came to the Nahanni Country in 1927. Red Pant, the natives called him, because he always wore distinctive, heavy trousers of scarlet stroud. His driving ambition was to find gold – a dream that never came to fruition in 46 years of searching up the South Nahanni and Flat rivers. Despite the deaths of other prospectors and the enveloping sense of foreboding and mystery, Faille made the Nahanni his home. At times he was given up for dead. Yet, inevitably, he would show up once again at Fort Simpson for supplies. One spring on the way out he met two Mounties looking for him. "Each one had a shovel. They'd come to bury me,"[31] recalled Faille.

Out of his obsession grew the Faille legend. Folklore has it that he once broke his back in a fall while alone far up the South Nahanni River. "Faille was as tough as a wolverine ... probably a little tougher,"[32] noted his friend Fred Sibbeston. The injured Faille crawled to his isolated cabin where he survived by drinking water from melting icicles and eating what little food he had on hand. Eventually, his back healed but at a permanently bent angle. Later, when his teeth came loose from scurvy, he pulled four of them out with a pair of pliers. By the time he died at Fort Simpson in 1974 he had become a larger-than-life character whose exploits were well documented in magazine articles, books, and feature films.

Another famous figure whose name is indelibly linked to the Nahanni region is Raymond M. Patterson, an Oxford scholar and adventurer. Like Faille, Patterson first ventured up the South Nahanni River in 1927 in search of gold. Unlike Faille, Patterson spent only a few years roaming the Nahanni Country. However, what he saw and experienced inspired him later to write a wonderful, classic tale of wilderness adventure called *The Dangerous River*. A great communicator and a vivid author, Patterson did much to bring the colour, beauty, and spirit of the Nahanni to people around the world. It was he, perhaps more than anyone, who helped dispel the prevailing attitude that the South Nahanni was 'straight suicide,' a place to be avoided.

In 1930, near the beginning of the Great Depression, yet another notable and adventuresome young man, Dick Turner, came to the Nahanni, drawn by its promise of abundant fur-bearing animals. A strong and determined person, he brought his lovely bride, Vera, to the wilderness of this challenging north country where, working side by side, they made a home for themselves and raised four children. Turner was a man who responded to the changing times. He had many careers and was truly a jack-of-all-trades. Among other things, at one time or another, he was a trapper, wood cutter, prospector, independent trader, riverman, magistrate, and bush pilot. A keen observer and a skilled storyteller, Turner went on to write several excellent books, including *Nahanni* and *Wings of the North*, that tell of decades of life and experience in the Nahanni region.

The talk of a third Nahanni gold rush in 1933 attracted a fourth character, Gus Kraus, to Fort Simpson. As with so many others, Kraus headed up the Flat River to search for that elusive yellow metal.

Poling up The Splits of the South Nahanni River, 1928

Along Bennett Creek, a tributary, Kraus and his partners came across old sluice boxes, shovels, and picks. Kraus was certain that these belonged to the ill-fated McLeod brothers and that in this area they had once found placer gold. Like Faille and Turner, Kraus spent a lifetime prospecting and trapping in the Nahanni wilderness, assisted much of the time by Mary, his capable Dene wife. For many years the Krauses lived by the thermal pools below First Canyon on the South Nahanni River. Their old home-site is now known as Kraus Hot Springs. Gus himself, through his long association with these sulphureous springs, became known as Stinking Water Man to the Dene. In 1971, when land including the hot springs was set aside for the establishment of the Nahanni National Park Reserve, Gus and Mary moved to the magnificent setting of Little Doctor Lake.

Albert Faille, Raymond Patterson, Dick Turner, and Gus Kraus are the more colourful and memorable of the many white people who came to the Nahanni region during the first few decades of the twentieth century. Among the local Dene and Metis there were also several prominent old-timers who are not as well known to the outside world, if at all. In the North, however, these individuals are highly respected and admired to this day.

Charles Yohin, George Sibbeston, Joseph Cli, and John Tetso were outstanding Dene hunters and trappers, whose cunning and skill have fed many a hungry mouth. Their experience in the ways of the bush, their knowledge of Indian medicine, and their status in the communities are still talked about and fondly remembered. These esteemed bushmen are commemorated by the names given to lakes found in the areas where they trapped and hunted.

Towering above all of them was Ted Trindell, a skilled Metis trapper, dog driver, and woodsman. "Ted was a real bushman of the old type. There were others like him, but he was unique in that he could express that life so well and with so much imagery."[33] Over the course of a long life, he became an acclaimed storyteller and philosopher. Trindell was an accomplished speaker, fluent in English, French, and several Dene languages. He was witness to a culture at the most profound point of its transformation and spoke knowingly of the concerns of the Metis and Dene. "He was one of the few men of the region who still had a full command of the Indian culture and lore which sustained life prior to and during the encroachment of southern values."[34]

Nothing epitomized the changing times, which locals such as Ted Trindell and Charles Yohin witnessed, more than the colonial comforts that were then enjoyed by the staff of the Hudson's Bay Company. While the remote country of the mountains and canyons remained beyond the pale of civilization, the forts in the lowlands along the Mackenzie and Liard rivers were increasingly assuming the trappings of white man's society.

At Fort Simpson, the Hudson's Bay men whiled away the long winter evenings, sociably smoking their pipes, reading volumes housed in the extensive library, having philosophical discussions, and playing chess, checkers, cards, and billiards. A Chief Factor, Julian Camsell, had imported the billiard table at great cost and labour from England. His son Charles, who later served as the Commissioner of the Northwest Territories, remembered the "hell" of playing billiards with elliptical home-made balls. "[O]ne winter when new balls did not arrive with the year's outfit, an attempt was made by the steamboat engineers to turn balls on a lathe out of mammoth ivory some hundreds or thousands of years old. ... This ivory in the form of tusks could be found here and there over the north country and there was one room in our house full of the tusks as well as bones of the mammoth."[35]

Talk in the winter of 1920-1921 was of oil discovered on Bear Island in the Mackenzie River below Fort Norman and of the coming treaty with the Dene. It was to be an unusual year that, for a while, quickened the pace of quiet life along the Mackenzie. In January thirteen dog teams pulled into Fort Simpson, carrying men and their outfits who were headed downriver in the rush to stake oil claims. In March the first airplanes came to the Northwest Territories – two Imperial Oil Junkers, which flew over Fort Simpson and then landed on a field near the Hudson's Bay Post. In June, well before the first steamer arrived, 92 boats of every description, carrying oil prospectors and speculators, passed by on the way north to Fort Norman. And in July the Treaty Commissioner, Henry A. Conroy, arrived by houseboat.

The Canadian government considered the idea of a treaty with the natives of the Mackenzie Valley as early as 1891. However, this

Above: *Albert Faille at his Flat River Cabin Near Irvine Creek, 1927*
Below: *Edward Boostrum and Drying Rabbit Meat for Dog Food, 1923*

Above: *Albert Faille in Later Years Panning for Gold*
Below: *Trapper Ole Lindberg, His Son Edwin, and Herb Kerr, Blackstone, 1935*

notion faded away because the land was perceived to have no particular economic value. In 1920 this attitude changed abruptly in ten dramatic minutes during which a "column of oil spouted from the 6-inch casing to a height of 75 feet above the derrick floor, after which the well was capped."[36] The purported 'Biggest Oil Field in the World' near Fort Norman gave the government the impetus to "take a surrender of this territory from the Northern Chiefs as soon as possible in order to avoid complications with respect to the exploitation of the country for oil."[37]

With a sense of urgency, the terms and conditions of Treaty 11 were hastily drafted in Ottawa. Henry A. Conroy, an honest, big-hearted inspector with the Department of Indian Affairs, who had known and visited the Dene of the Mackenzie since 1907, was selected to lead the Royal Commission. Conroy received a copy of the Treaty with these instructions: "You should be guided by the terms set forth therein and ... no outside promises should be made by you to the Indians."[38] Conroy's duties were clear. He was not to negotiate a treaty; he was to impose a treaty. His role was merely to "obtain the consent and signatures of the Indian people of the Mackenzie District."[39]

Much controversy surrounds Treaty 11. Although the Dene raised concerns during the discussions, it is apparent that most of the natives did not fully understand the implications of the treaty. Many did not speak English, and verbal translations were rough. Reserves of land, although stipulated in writing, never materialized. Verbal promises would be broken. Ted Trindell was present at the negotiations and later testified, "The Indians didn't know what treaty was. ... The Treaty party told them that they could carry on hunting as they wished. But then again in the Treaty book it says that you'll be subject to the law, and it says that after the Treaty you had to abide by whatever rules came along, but at Treaty time the Treaty party didn't tell them that. It was still your country. The Treaty was more or less to keep peace in the family. In fact the Indians didn't realize that they were signing their rights over. ... The Indian was smart in the bush, but as far as civilization was concerned, he had no more idea than a two-year-old baby."[40]

So in the summer of 1921 the native people of the Mackenzie River near Fort Simpson, and the following year those of the Liard

River who traded at Fort Liard, ceded their claim to the region, including the Nahanni Country. From this point onward the Dene were bound by the rules and regulations of Canadian jurisdiction.

The federal government did not hesitate to legislate laws to control the northern fur trade. By this time the native people had been exposed to the trade for 120 years. Along with hunting and fishing, trapping had become a traditional activity. An attempt was made to protect the livelihood of the Dene by discouraging the influx of white trappers moving into the area. Trapping licences were issued, and the fee levied for non-residents was high. In the face of soaring fur prices, this attempt proved ineffective. By 1926 there were so many trappers, and consequently a great number of competitive, independent trading posts, that it became necessary to institute a system of licensing the traders as well. Not too much time had passed before a tax was imposed on furs leaving the Northwest Territories, and a series of closed seasons was established on various game species that showed serious signs of overharvesting. Continued concern for the conservation of fur-bearers led to the creation of preserves where only the Dene were permitted to hunt and trap. One of these, the Mackenzie Mountains Game Preserve, encompassed the entire South Nahanni River drainage basin.

During the 1930s, 45 new trading posts opened along the Mackenzie River. However, these outposts were short-lived. Toward the end of the decade, fur prices crashed, and the effects of the Depression reached the Mackenzie Valley. In the aftermath, of all the trading firms, only the Hudson's Bay Company survived. Low fur prices continued into and following World War II. This sustained decline coupled with rising equipment costs signalled the end of the traditional fur trade era in the Mackenzie Valley.

A great number of the newcomers, who came to the North lured by tales of gold and fur, arrived on paddle-wheel steamboats, such as the *S.S. Mackenzie River* and the *S.S. Distributor*. By the 1920s one could travel with relative ease from Edmonton to Fort Simpson and even transfer onward to Nahanni Butte and Fort Liard.

The arrival of the steamboats was an exciting event. The mood at the forts was particularly buoyant in spring. With the lengthening days, the ice in the rivers breaking up, and the return of the migratory waterfowl, spirits were high. Soon the Hudson's Bay Company

Raymond Patterson in the South Nahanni Canyons, 1928

Above: *Summer on the Mackenzie, the* S.S. Mackenzie River *and the* S.S. Distributor
Below: *Chief Antoine Nakekon* (sixth from left) *and Other Dene Men at Fort Simpson, 1925*

boat would appear from upriver, bringing supplies and mail from the south. With the steamboats, too, came music, dances, gambling, and fine food. Fred Sibbeston, an elder at Fort Simpson, remembered when "every man and his dog would wait on the bank for the steamer."[41]

In early July, on its first run of the year, the *Distributor*, affectionately called The Great Smell, would arrive in Fort Simpson. Even before the vessel was spotted, the fragrance of oranges and apples, mixed with the barn-yard smells of chickens and cattle, tantalized the nostrils of those on shore. "It would smell like everything. Some days if the wind was right, it would smell like an orchard. Ten months out of the year we wouldn't see an orange ... and when they did come, you could smell them a long way off,"[42] recalled Bill Lafferty, son of Jonas Lafferty.

Jonas, one of the finest Mackenzie River pilots, guided the *Distributor* for many years. He never ran a boat aground and was still called out at 76 years of age. Jonas piloted during the era before channel markers were introduced. All the landmarks for the 1,100-mile journey between Fort Smith and Aklavik were committed to memory. Pilots came to recognize how sounds reverberated from the shore so as to enable them to know where they were when travelling in the dark and also when enveloped in fog. They learned to read the water. The smallest ripple had meaning and could indicate the location of a shifting sand-bar just beneath the surface.

The steamboats generally stopped at each trading post for several festive days while supplies were unloaded and bales of fur were taken aboard. In 1928, however, the *Distributor* unwittingly became the carrier of misery and death.

Philip H. Godsell, the inspector of the Hudson's Bay Company, was a passenger on the *Distributor* that summer. He noted that "just as the *Distributor* was loading up for her first trip to the Arctic, [two fellows I knew] arrived back from Edmonton where they had gone to sell their furs. A few days later they became quite sick; just a cold thought everybody and let it go at that. Hardly, however, had the steamer commenced to work her way down river ere David McPherson, the veteran pilot, was taken very ill and by the time I stepped ashore at Hay River there were quite a number of sick on board. Then as the travelling plague spot, which the *Distributor* had unknowingly become, went cruising on her way she left behind at

Above: *Bales of Fur at Fort Simpson*
Below: *Barge Pushed by the* S.S. Distributor, *1928*

59

Above: *Dick Turner Standing by Old Claim Stake, 1966*
Below: *Albert Faille in Later Years*

Above: *Gus and Mary Kraus, Kraus Hot Springs, 1962*
Below: *Ted Trindell, His Wife, Bella* (far right), *1930*

every post the germs of the disease. Twenty-four hours after her departure, the entire population of each settlement became prostrate with malignant flue, and ere it spent its force in the Delta nearly six hundred of the natives had gone to the Great Beyond."[43]

Without natural immunities to the disease and lacking medical supplies, the Dene suffered greatly. In a matter of weeks one in six natives perished. Elders and leaders were lost. Children were orphaned. The toll had been heavy in previous epidemics but nothing compared to the horror experienced throughout the Mackenzie Valley that summer of 1928.

"White man's sickness. All Indian sick. Some die, me pretty soon, too," moaned Drybone to Helge Ingstad, a Norwegian. Ingstad entered in his journal that sad day, "I go from teepee to teepee, and a most sorrowful spectacle meets my gaze. On the bare earth strewn with spruce twigs lie the huddled forms of the sick – men, women, and children, wrapped up in skins and filthy rags. They are shivering although the air is stifling inside, and they cough up blood and stare at me with strange eyes. Off in the woods I find three corpses, covered over with aspen leaves."[44]

The proud, independent Dene people were ravaged by disease. Their culture was changing significantly, and an age-old way of life in the North was passing swiftly. Increasingly the natives built permanent homes at the trading posts, which were becoming established settlements. The fur trade, which had grown into such an important part of their annual subsistence cycle, was declining. Government deemed it necessary to play an ever-greater role in controlling northern affairs and the lives of the people who lived there. The self-reliance and sense of complete freedom that the natives had enjoyed, and that so many early white adventurers had sought, would soon disappear forever.

In his later years, Raymond Patterson eloquently expressed his thoughts about his own experiences on the South Nahanni River – thoughts that reflect upon a passing era. "Those of us who had the good fortune to be on the South Nahanni in those last days of the old North may, in times of hunger or hardship, have cursed the day we ever heard the name of that fabled river. Yet a treasure was ours in the end; memories of a carefree time and an utter and absolute freedom, which the years cannot dim nor the present age provide."[45]

Raymond Patterson, 1966

Above: *Junkers Monoplane, the* Vic, *on Floats, May 1921*
Below: *Western Canadian Airways Planes at Fort Simpson, pre-1930*

6

THE BUSH PILOTS

George Gorman peered down at the island of Fort Simpson from the open cockpit of the *Rene*, a F-13 Junkers monoplane. It was a cold winter's day, March 28, 1921. Through frosted goggles he could plainly see a jagged jumble of ice-flows on the frozen Mackenzie River where he had hoped to land. Signalling to Elmer Fullerton in the *Vic*, a second Junkers, Gorman circled and descended towards a smoother-looking field near the Hudson's Bay Post. Amid the cheers and waves of excited onlookers, the *Rene* touched down, only to plough straight into a rock-hard snowdrift that tore away her landing gear and shattered a ski and the propeller. Fullerton, watching from above, selected a safer landing spot and came in without incident.

The *Vic* and the *Rene*, owned by the Imperial Oil Company, were the first aircraft to fly into the Northwest Territories. The planes were headed for the site of the oil discovery near Fort Norman. Unfortunately, all efforts to get the damaged *Rene* airborne met with failure. The hapless Gorman crashed the *Rene* two more times, shattering another propeller, breaking a second ski, and bending a wing. By this time, a month had slipped by. With the weather warming and spring break-up imminent, all hope of reaching Fort Norman on ski-equipped planes was abandoned. Leaving the *Rene* to be repaired later, the *Vic* retreated south, driven by a temporary, home-made propeller that had been fashioned from oak sleigh boards laminated with moose hide and hoof glue. It would be late May before the *Vic*, outfitted with pontoons, returned to the Mackenzie Valley.

The episode of the *Vic* and the *Rene* was not an auspicious beginning for the use of aircraft in the North. However, before too long the airplane became an indispensable part of northern life, shortening trips that took weeks or even months by canoe or dog team to only a few hours or days. By the 1930s, scheduled flights along the Mackenzie River corridor were common.

This was the period of 'seat-of-the-pants flying.' There were no radios and no weather forecasts. This was the leather helmet and goggle era when pilots battled the elements in open cockpits; when stop-overs in winter necessitated the immediate draining of engine oil, which was reheated and carefully poured back into the crankcase just prior to take-off. This was a time when maps were woefully inadequate. Large areas, including the entire North and South Nahanni watersheds, were simply marked Unknown, demanding that pilots be cartographers and explorers as well.

A few of the early northern flyers took prospectors up through the canyons of the South Nahanni River, veering left at Direction Mountain, which indicated the route to the hoped-for Flat River gold fields. Among the first bush pilots to pioneer flight paths into the Nahanni mountains was Wilfred 'Wop' May, the World War I Flying Ace who had the dubious distinction of being the greenhorn stalked by the Red Baron when the latter was fatally shot down. Wop May, his contemporaries Punch Dickens, Stan McMillan, Leigh Britnell, and 'Doc' Oaks, and later George Dalziel and Dick Turner, quickly learned that flying in the mountains required a rule book all its own.

These men operated in the days before much was known about mountain flying. There were a lot of scary stories – fly a mile, learn a mile. Those who had the ability to sense danger and stay away from it survived. The lives of a number of pilots and their passengers have been claimed by the Nahanni, with its rugged topography, blind canyons, and unstable weather. On the map today such names as Death Lake, Stall Gorge, Crash Canyon, the Funeral Range, and the Sombre Mountains bear witness to past tragedies.

Pilots joke about the dangers presented by cumulo-granite – dense, fluffy clouds containing rock. But reality is that the combination of bad weather and disorientation can kill. Mountain flying, of necessity, is based on visual references, and, when storm clouds move in and visibility decreases, much of the landscape can look the same. In a land where passes through the mountains and canyons are few and tight, where there is one right route and nine wrong ones, and where fuel is always a major concern, getting lost in poor weather can be deadly. As Dick Turner, who flew from his

Wop May, World War I Flying Ace and Legendary Bush Pilot

home at Nahanni Butte for many years, advised, "If a situation starts to develop that you cannot handle, you get the hell out of there; you land or go home. Don't be proud; pride and heroes are buried together in the same grave."[46]

Fixed-wing and helicopter pilots who service the Nahanni Country today are well trained in the techniques of mountain flying. Okanagan Helicopters, for example, offers the finest mountain flying program available anywhere in the world. And senior, experienced flyers, such as Jim Broadbent, make a point of passing along the practical knowledge they have acquired over the years. Much of this advice is based on simple principles and common sense.

Ron Sprang, a veteran bush pilot with Simpson Air, says that when flying in tight quarters the hardest thing to teach new pilots is the necessity of staying close to the walls of canyons and valleys. "You fly so tight that you can count the lice on the back of squirrels. ... Seriously, what I mean is that you should be close enough to see the individual cones on spruce trees. Then you know that, if the need arises, you have all the room that is available to turn."[47] Another experienced flyer, Mansell Patterson, adds that "pilots should fly down the shaded side of canyons and turn into the sun to take full advantage of natural thermal lift."[48] Pete Cowie is a living legend and one of the first commercial bush pilots to operate year round from Fort Simpson. He says it can be difficult to judge the depth of water in an unfamiliar lake from the air so as to determine if it is safe to land a float plane. Pete looks for signs, "You can always land a plane on lily pads, provided the lake is long enough to get in and out of. Water lilies grow only where the depth is sufficient to protect their roots from freezing in winter. Where there are lily pads, there's just enough water to safely land a plane. When I haul trappers out to a strange lake, I just head for the lily pads."[49] A swimming moose is another indicator of water that is adequately deep for landing. Pete cautions not to be misled by a standing moose, even if the beast is submerged up to its belly. Quite likely, the moose is knee deep in muck and the lake is probably too shallow.

Bush pilots all have stories of past experiences and mishaps, some humorous, others positively hair-raising. One time, a trapper flying with Mansell Patterson was checking his gun, which he claimed was empty. No sooner had he said this when, in mid-air, the gun discharged and blew a hole through the roof of the plane, scaring Mansell half to death. Pete Cowie still chuckles when he thinks of a radio call he received from Louis Norwegian, asking that he fly to Jean Marie and pick up some people. It was spring break-up, but Louis assured him that a smooth, straight airstrip had been marked out with spruce trees on the still-frozen Mackenzie River. "So I flew over, and I saw the trees all in a row ending right at the edge of this mess of open water. 'That's kind of short,' I thought. Because of the wind I had to land going out from shore. I came in as tight and slow as I could. After touching down I knew I wasn't going to stop the plane on skis before plunging into that open water. So I kicked hard left rudder and spun her round with a burst of power and taxied back. 'Louis,' I said, 'she's smooth enough, but damn she's kind of short.' 'Yah,' he said, 'as a matter of fact, half of it floated away this morning after I gave you the call.'"[50]

Planes and helicopters are the taxis, cars, and trucks of the outlying arctic and subarctic communities. Without the skilled and knowledgeable pilots and the aircraft they fly, the North as it is today would come to a grinding halt. The aviation industry supplies many essential services: hauling in groceries, freight, and mail; evacuating emergency medical cases; and delivering water and fuel needed to fight forest fires. It is also involved with tourism, policing, pipeline patrols, water survey projects, and numerous wildlife and geological studies.

Today's world of schedules, safety concerns, and efficient service has all but eroded the aura of danger, romance, and glamour that once was associated with the early bush pilots. Charter operators who own one or more light aircraft face long hours, horrendous insurance rates, and narrow profit margins. Survival in this business requires a high degree of economic bravery as well as physical courage. It takes more than simply being a skilled pilot. Operators, such as Ted Grant of Simpson Air, find it helpful to take on many roles: bush pilot, businessman, politician, promoter, and tour guide, to name but a few.

But talk to these flyers about the mountains or fly with them into the Nahanni – that wilderness of peaks, canyons, hidden lakes, and turbulent rivers – and you will see their eyes light up. It is a land unencumbered by air traffic and control towers, a land they love and know like the back of their hands.

Above: *Pete Cowie, Veteran Bush Pilot*
Below: *Ted Grant* (standing) *and His Cessna 185, Rabbitkettle Lake*

George Pellissey, A Mountain Dene

Bill Lafferty, A Metis Trapper

Late one lazy Autumn day we nosed our canoe into a small cove by a low cut-bank on the Liard River. Over a year of extensive travel, exploration, and high adventure in this unique corner of the Earth was drawing to a close. Soon we would be enveloped by another world, one of schedules and deadlines, of hustle and bustle, and of noise and pollution – all of which seemed unappealing and somewhat threatening as we pitched our tent beneath a golden canopy of Trembling Aspen at the edge of the evening river.

Seated together on a log by our camp-fire, we watched the sun dip below the crest of snow-capped mountains. We were soothed by the muted murmur of the mighty Liard and experienced a deep sense of serenity in the presence of so many natural things. Again, the words of Raymond Patterson came to us: "We had been allowed to live for a little time in a world apart – a lonely world of surpassing beauty, that had given us all things from the sombre magnificence of the canyons to the gay sunshine of those wind-swept uplands; from the quiet of the dry side canyons to the uproar of the broken waters – a land where men pass, and the silence falls back into place behind them."[51]

As dusk settled and stars winked in the darkening vault of the heavens, we reflected on our own intense need for wild and silent

Rescue of Stranded Canoeists, the Rock Gardens, Upper South Nahanni River

places; for country, such as the Nahanni, where Nature reigns supreme and Man does not dominate; for land that is unfettered and unaffected by the developers, the dam builders, and the loggers.

On all fronts, the mounting pressures of industrial expansion and over-population are threatening the Earth's few remaining wilderness areas. If unchecked, how long will it be until there is no chance to be alone, before there is no quietness anywhere, and the call of birds, the rustle of leaves, and the sigh of the wind is drowned beneath the screeching din of civilization?

We continually hear talk about the need for economic growth to generate jobs, income, and material wealth, thereby improving the quality of life for the ever-expanding mass of humanity. If the economy takes a down-turn, if stock prices fall, if a few businesses go under, there is uncertainty, fear, even panic. But what of the wilderness? Where is the equal concern for what is happening to the plants, birds, animals, soil, water, and air?

Inevitably, all this growth and expansion occurs at the expense of the natural environment. Billions of dollars are spent on the acquisition of arms and on industrial incentives and bail-outs. Yet, while another commission reviews environmental concerns, our forests and wildlife continue to die, our water becomes more polluted, and our air gets harder to breath. According to the World Wildlife Fund, three wildlife species become extinct every day. Soon it will be one species per hour, increasing at an ever-greater rate. Ardent preservationist Robert Bateman says, "It is dangerous and sacrilegious what we are doing to our planet. It took billions of years for the Earth to become the marvellously rich, intricate, and complex place that exists today with all of its diversity and potential. During this century we are actively reducing and wiping out the variety and replacing it with a bland uniformity. It is 'say good-bye time' for much of our natural and human heritage." Only through the concern and efforts of everyone can the little wilderness left on Earth be preserved. The individual can help by pressuring politicians and supporting such organizations as the World Wildlife Fund, the Sierra Club, and the Canadian Parks and Wilderness Society.

That night in the Nahanni Country, by the fading embers of the camp-fire, our thoughts wandered from the magnificence of the land and the importance of wilderness preservation, to the aboriginal Dene who have inhabited this region since time immemorial. These native people never sought to alter their environment, but rather they lived for thousands of years in harmony with it, until the relatively recent encroachment of southern industrial values. There is a lesson here!

We thought of our friends George Pellessey, a Mountain Dene, who showed us how to build an efficient refrigerator with woven willow boughs spread above a cold mountain stream, and of Bill Lafferty, a Metis trapper, who entertained us with colourful stories of river pilots and life in the bush. Men such as these are at home in the mountains and are comfortable with the ways of the wild. They retain a knowledge of age-old skills, which are rapidly disappearing among the younger generation. It is this heritage, the traditional Dene values and skills, their way of life, that Dene leaders today wish to protect and preserve. They want their own culture to occupy an honourable place in the contemporary life of Canada, and they seek the right to determine their own future and the use of their land.

Whereas this north country is home to the Dene, it is a magnet, a dream destination, for many southerners who crave unspoiled and seemingly endless wilderness, clean rivers and lakes, and abundant wildlife. To those who have the skill and are prepared for the hazards associated with extremes of climate and terrain, and the inherent isolation, wilderness regions such as the Nahanni offer a unique challenge and an experience of a lifetime.

Many, perhaps most people, have a need for wilderness in some form, but the majority may never have the opportunity to experience the truly wild and remote places. For some of these men and women, it is enough that the promise remains. They take solace in the knowledge that these wild regions still exist and that perhaps one day they, too, or their children may awaken to find Grizzly bear tracks through their water-hole at dawn, see an eagle's feathers ruffle in the wind, and hear the howl of a wolf echo through the canyons at dusk.

This book celebrates just such a place – the Nahanni. The plates that follow reflect Nature's supremacy. Man enters the picture only as a small, insignificant figure, dwarfed by the immensity of the land. May the relationship always be so.

Pat and Rosemarie Keough
Little Doctor Lake, Northwest Territories

PLATES AND COMMENTARIES

PLATE 11   *Ancient Dall Sheep Skulls, Grotte Valerie Cave – September 1987*

PLATE 12   *Short-billed Dowitcher in the Sedges – June 1987*

We came to the Moose Ponds in springtime when the first, fresh, green shoots were showing on the floating mats of sedge and along the marshy shores of these shallow lakes. We were thrilled by the variety and abundance of bird life. A pair of Bald Eagles regularly patrolled the great alpine valley in the shadow of Mount Wilson, searching for prey to take back to hungry mouths in the nest. The Common Loon and the beautiful Red-throated Loon were at home here, and the hills echoed their haunting calls. We were amused by the antics of the small Red-necked Phalarope and the courtship performance of the Common Snipe in its high-flying display that results in a hollow tremolo hu-hu-hu sound. Semipalmated Plovers zipped about on the mud flats, and a pair of Arctic Terns hovered and plunged near the gravel beach at the mouth of a small, snow-fed mountain stream. The graceful silhouettes of Trumpeter Swans were to be seen, as well as numerous species of duck. On more than one occasion we were startled as Willow Ptarmigan exploded from underfoot. The Moose Ponds are indeed a birdwatcher's dream.

One evening, while quietly paddling our canoe through the sedge, we spotted this Short-billed Dowitcher feeding along the shoreline. Its long, straight bill was probing the mud with a rapid, jabbing motion. When the bird saw us, it paused briefly, allowing us to capture this image.

Another day we beached our canoe on a low, grassy bank below Mount Wilson. We enjoyed the view across the water toward the distant peaks and Mount Christie. Flowing out of these mountains and down the valley through the Moose Ponds is a small, clear, cold, tumbling stream – the headwaters of the legendary South Nahanni River. This stream and these Moose Ponds are the starting point of many an unforgettable whitewater canoeing adventure.

PLATE 13 *Near the Headwaters of the South Nahanni River – June 1987*

PLATE 14   *Fireweed, New Life in the Burn – July 1987*

PLATE 15   *The Winding North Nahanni River – December 1987*

PLATE 16   *Sunrise, The Nahanni Range – August 1987*

The rising sun paints clouds with gold, as Nature composes a symphony of colour over the valley of the Tetcela River and the dark, distant peaks of the Nahanni Range.

Three days before, the weather had been warm and promising, pleasant for hiking, climbing, and just enjoying the spectacular scenery. We had camped high above the tree-line on the wind-swept Nahanni Plateau while exploring the country between the South Nahanni River and Death Canyon. About mid-morning, as we were breaking camp, we noticed a peculiar silver-grey mist creeping towards us up the canyons and low over the plateau. At the same time we heard a distant, muted, moaning sound. Always expecting the unexpected, we knew something was afoot with the weather – probably something unpleasant for us.

Whenever we make camp, especially above the tree-line, we keep our eyes open for a safe, secure retreat should the need arise. On this day we quickly headed for a nearby 10-foot-deep solution depression – a small karst street in the flat limestone top of the Nahanni Plateau. We had barely gained this shelter when the wind hit like a hammer, driving shrapnel-like pellets of frozen ice. In an incredibly short span of 10 minutes, the temperature plummeted from 65 degrees fahrenheit to three below zero. Above our refuge, a full-blown blizzard, with screaming winds and horizontal driving snow, was in progress. To have been caught unprepared on the open plateau in white-out conditions, with sheer cliffs all around and where the wind-chill was at least 30 below, would have spelt certain death.

We huddled there for three days, waiting for the storm to blow itself out. We were secure and warm with our sleeping bags, small tent, and portable stove. Now, on a new morning, as we crawled from our tent, this beautiful scene was spread before us – the sun burning away the mist that concealed the lovely valley below. It was the start of a friendlier, warmer, summer day.

PLATE 17   *At the Edge, Third Canyon – July 1987*

A crumbling limestone outcrop offers a breath-taking vantage point for a view of Third Canyon and the South Nahanni River far below. Rather than showing the river itself and more of the canyon, we focused instead on a section of the towering cliff face and the void beyond. The vertical wall of rock running top to bottom through our photograph, the small figure on the ledge, and the distant trees help create a sense of height and immensity. This feeling is indeed appropriate, for the great canyons of the Nahanni Country are among the deepest on Earth.

We ferried across from our island camp-site and climbed a cut-bank to better enjoy the scene. Far away up the river, we could still see Mount Wilson under threatening clouds.

An island camp-site can be a place of mixed blessings on a river such as the South Nahanni. Islands are generally low lying and offer an advantage for loading and unloading heavy canoes. But one should beware of storms in distant mountain valleys that can cause this river to rise up to six feet in less than an hour. Many trippers have awakened to soggy sleeping bags, as the rapidly rising river sent them scrambling to prevent food packs and canoes from being swept away.

When camped on shingle bars or low islands, the canoe should be secured to a well-rooted tree, willow bush, or large rock. If none of these are available then, as adventurer R.M. Patterson used to do, tie the canoe to the sleeping bag or, as we have done, to the tent poles. Then, if the canoe goes, at least you will be going with it.

On this occasion, our stay was uneventful. But on a subsequent canoe trip, we found the island greatly modified. It had been radically reduced in size, altered in shape with channels cut through it, and swept clear of all vegetation – changes that attest to the power of the rampaging river.

PLATE 18   *Camp-site, Upper South Nahanni River — August 1984*

PLATE 21   *A Winter Swim, Kraus Hot Springs – December 1987*

PLATE 22   *Luxuriant Cow Parsnip, Moore's Hot Springs – July 1987*

Up there, on the rim of the Arctic Circle, was a tropical valley; a mist-enshrouded notch in the earth that had escaped the impact of the Ice Age. A steam-heated oasis shut off from polar blasts by towering mountain ranges capped with everlasting snow where mighty dinosaurs and monsters of a forgotten age still disported themselves in steaming pools girth with rich and luxuriant vegetation ... ."[52]

Until recent times, fanciful tales, such as this rambling yarn of an old trapper and the imaginative writings of journalists and other storytellers, helped perpetuate the myth of tropical valleys hidden away in the remote Nahanni mountains and canyons. What do exist are several hundred hot springs. Some are quite small; others large, such as Kraus Hot Springs, Moore's Hot Springs, and those at Hole-in-the-Wall Lake.

There may not be dinosaurs, but there are beaver at Kraus Hot Springs where we had stopped for a swim after skiing. The beaver that fell the large poplars bridging the warm stream have the luxury of living in thermal-heated pools and lodges year round. Here, hot water, at an average of 100 degrees fahrenheit, boils up through the sand and gravel alluvium. In winter, steam rising from the water rimes every branch and each blade of grass with a delicate white covering of frost. At other times of the year, vegetation growing in the warm, moist atmosphere is rich and luxuriant. Wild Cow Parsnip thrives by Moore's Hot Spring and reaches a height of over seven feet.

Indians of old believed the waters had soothing, healing qualities that were beneficial for aching bones. We found this was so, having stopped many times by these hot pools to warm our weary bodies at the end of a long day.

PLATE 23   *Mouldering Log Cabins – September 1987*

One rainy autumn day we were visiting with Vera Turner in the lovely log house she and Dick had built on the bank of the Liard River near Blackstone. We were talking of times past, the old days, the old ways, and the larger-than-life characters who were drawn to this remote North country. It was still drizzling later when she directed us along the river bank to the long-abandoned Lindburg homestead. Here, in a melancholy setting we took this picture, which for us is evocative of the numerous, old log cabins mouldering away, forgotten, along the rivers and streams of the Nahanni Country.

The Mackenzie Lowlands stretch to the horizon east of the Nahanni and Liard ranges. In the fall large, golden groves of Trembling Aspen can be seen everywhere, their straight, chalk-white trunks reaching for the sky. These are pioneering trees, usually the first to colonize a region. Growing in their shade, secondary trees, such as the White Spruce, become established. We made this photograph one of just trunks, as their bold, splayed pattern, with gold and green accents, caught our eye.

PLATE 24   *Patterns in an Aspen Grove – September 1987*

PLATE 25   *Hiking in the Ragged Range – September 1987*

PLATE 26   *Azure Mountain Jewels, Meltwater Pools – July 1987*

PLATE 27 *Frost on Cabin Window, Little Doctor Lake – March 1987*

PLATE 28   *Old Woman and Tepees, The Flats, Fort Simpson — September 1987*

PLATE 29   *The Rock Gardens, South Nahanni River – August 1984*

"A fantastic but most dangerous trip. There were numerous attacks on our canoes by floating rocks ... ."[53] So wrote a modern-day adventurer after a trip through the upper South Nahanni's infamous Rock Gardens. Indeed, when running this thrilling whitewater labyrinth, we often find it difficult to tell just what is and what is not moving. At times, all is a blur of motion – rocks, water, foam, flashing paddles, the canoe dipping and diving, your partner reaching and straining. Here, canoeists thread their way through the rapids known as the Eye-of-the-Needle.

The Little Nahanni River snakes through the hills towards Third Canyon and its meeting with the South Nahanni River near the distant Backbone Range. The tranquil beauty of the river, as seen from this perspective high on a mountain ridge, belies the fact that it, too, is an adrenaline-pumping whitewater river that has eaten more than one canoe.

At times of flood and especially during spring run-off, many of these fast-moving mountain rivers carry boulders along with them. Some of these boulders are considerable and rather astonishing in size. More than once, as we stood on shore, we heard the dull thud and thump of boulders bouncing and banging against one another as the current carried them along the river-bed. Centuries of such wearing action have resulted in the familiar smooth-rounded features of these rocks, which can be thankfully forgiving to the canoe that inadvertently side-swipes one of them.

PLATE 31   *Rappel Cenote, Cenote Col – August 1987*

PLATE 32 *The Raven Lake Stone Arches – August 1987*

The Nahanni karst is a region of unquestionable complexity and beauty that has been slowly sculpted through the ages by the persistent, dissolving action of rainwater falling onto and percolating through limestone. It is a jigsaw assemblage of spectacular, natural features that includes caves, rock bridges, sinkholes, isolated rock towers, solution streets, canyon systems, and extensive rock labyrinths. In fact, it is one of the most remarkable limestone landscapes found anywhere on Earth.

Edged with a rich carpet of pale yellow lichen, the deep, dark, and mysterious eye-like pool of Rappel Cenote appears to glower from the depths of the Earth. This vertical-walled sinkhole is just one example of some 23 similar depressions that can be found on a narrow limestone ridge known as Cenote Col. This pock-marked ridge, separating North and South Col Canyons, is a scant 300 yards long by 100 yards wide.

With a sense of anticipation and discovery, we set out to explore the area. Some of the sinkholes were quite large and resembled the infamous cenotes of Mexico's Yucatan Peninsula, which in times past the Maya used as sacrificial wells. We scrambled about, descending into one sinkhole, crawling through an underground passage, and emerging in yet another sinkhole. Others, such as Rappel Cenote, were filled with water. This water is actually melted snow that had drifted into the depressions, which act as snow traps during the winter. Ice-plugs in the subterranean drainage routes, a common characteristic of discontinuous permafrost, prevent the water from seeping away. In studying Rappel Cenote, we were amazed to realize that the water in the pool did not find its way through the scant 30-foot wall that separates it from the 300-foot drop into South Col Canyon.

Many wonders can be seen along the Raven Lake karst street. This street is actually a long, deep solutional corridor that formed along faults and joints in the limestone. Above Raven Lake we discovered these massive rock bridges. The arches are remnants of an ancient cave system. Long ago, great volumes of water flowed through these conduits to emerge at some far-off location as cold, clear springs. Today, White Spray Spring on the South Nahanni River and Bubbling Springs at the headwaters of the Sundog Creek are examples of such outlets.

PLATE 33   *Virginia Falls in Winter – March 1987*

PLATE 34 *Detail, Virginia Falls in Winter – March 1987*

PLATE 35   *Nature's Garden – August 1987*

PLATE 36   *Beautiful Death Lake, Nahanni Plateau – September 1987*

PLATE 37   *Along Sundog Creek – December 1987*

PLATE 38   *Cadillac International Airport, Prairie Creek – July 1987*

December in the mountains finds dusk settling by mid-afternoon. We were travelling up a branch of the Sundog Creek that flows out of a pass through the Tundra Ridge of the Nahanni Plateau. Arrangements had been made for Jim Broadbent of Okanagan Helicopters to pick us up near a lovely, frozen waterfall. It was time to leave the wilderness and head home for Christmas. Soon we heard the beat of chopper blades, and Jim swung into view. When you live out on the land for the better part of a year, as we have, you come to rely on, value, and deeply appreciate the friendliness, reliability, and tremendous skill of the northern mountain bush pilots. Flyers, such as Ted Grant, Ron Sprang, Jim Broadbent, and Frank Carmichael, who operate the planes and helicopters were our life-line. They resupplied us, moved our canoe and gear, and even picked up and dropped off film when required.

The main terminal building and pilots' lounge look...well...somewhat moth-eaten. But then, this is not your every-day, big-city commuter airport either. As the sign says, it is Cadillac International Airport, and it is up by Prairie Creek, on the edge of the Funeral Range. Pilots flying into this mountain airstrip, which is part of the moth-balled Cadillac Silver Mine, have to do some fancy twisting and turning round a few peaks and down a few valleys. However, this is nothing unusual for pilots used to flying over all types of terrain, often in foul weather.

The brightly coloured fuel drums are flown into the mountains at great expense. They may not be the most sightly things, but without a fuel cache one simply could not operate in this remote area.

Rainbows arching over great glacial erratics; see-forever views across deep, winding canyons; Golden Eagles riding thermals high above alpine plateaus; brilliant, minuscule flowers amid clumps of fossilized coral; Dall sheep, white dots on a distant, grey scree slope; a river meandering like a silver thread in the black folds of an evening valley; sounds of falling water from a distant, dark gorge; ground squirrels scampering through dew-dappled grass; a hike in clouds amid the indistinct shapes of a ghostly world; icy cold air spilling from a cave; Grizzly bear tracks in our water-hole at dawn; ...a kaleidoscope of images, sounds, and feelings – the magnificent Ram Plateau.

The Ram Plateau offers some of the finest hiking on alpine tundra that we have experienced anywhere. Not only is the walking extremely easy along the flat-topped, interconnected ridges of the plateau, but the views are always breath-taking. Many of the steep-walled canyons, with their deeply incised drainage channels, are over 3,000 feet deep. These awesome canyons, spires, and buttresses have been carved in massive beds of grey Nahanni limestone.

PLATE 41   *Early Morning, Common Loon Flexing Wings – June 1987*

PLATE 42   *Colourful Scree Slopes, The Backbone Range – July 1987*

PLATE 43   *Rabbitkettle Tufa Mound – August 1984*

PLATE 44   *Detail of Rimstone Dams, Rabbitkettle Tufa Mound – July 1987*

Like the spirit of an angry god, black rain clouds build towards the rimstone dams and the iron-red spillway of the north Rabbitkettle Tufa Mound. This beautiful, coral-coloured mound of soft crystalline rock continues to be formed by the precipitation of calcium and magnesium carbonate that are carried in the waters of a thermal spring. Actually, there are three springs and two distinct tufa mounds, which are located in the shadow of the Ragged Range at the edge of the Rabbitkettle River. These are the largest examples of this land feature known in Canada. The north mound, the finer and more active of the two, has a height of 47 feet and a diameter of 250 feet at its base. Warm water rises up through the mound, filling a vertical shaft of undetermined depth. The water spills out through a large orifice at a temperature of 65 degrees fahrenheit. It flows across the top of the mound and down its side on a relatively straight and narrow path, which rotates slowly like the hand of a huge clock. One rotation is estimated to take an entire century. This process occurs as numerous small pools, retained by tiny dams of rimstone, temporarily trap the mineralized water, thereby aiding the precipitation of tufa. As the rims of these pools increase in height, the water spills sideways to a new course, and dam building commences elsewhere. Thus, minutely, the fragile beauty that is the tufa mound grows year after year.

In days of old, the native people believed that a legendary figure named Yamoria determined when the kettle would be full of water. It was very bad luck when the kettle was empty and very good luck when it was full and overflowing. Offerings of food, and later bullets and cloth, were thrown into the orifice as a means of bringing good fortune to the people.

PLATE 45   *Red Squirrel in Spruce Tree – April 1987*

PLATE 46   *Glacier Lake in the Ragged Range – August 1984*

PLATE 47   *The Old Burn, A Maze of Fallen Trees – April 1987*

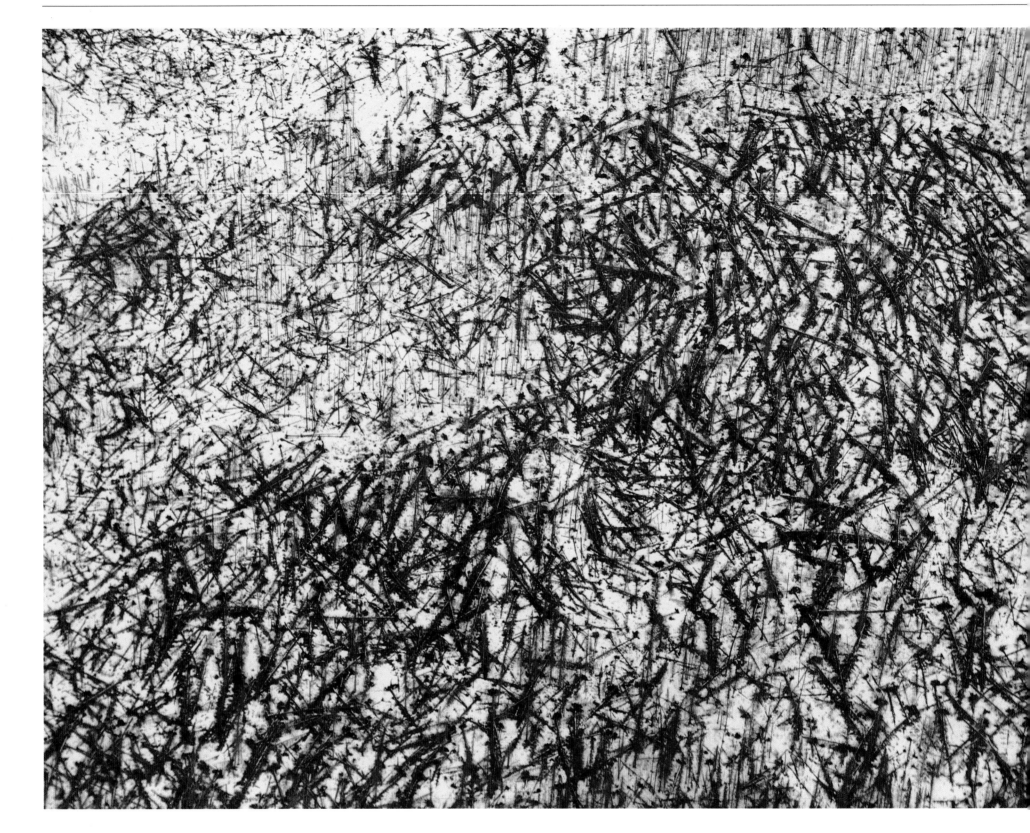

PLATE 48   *Cow Moose in the Moose Ponds – June 1987*

Looking like abstract art, the darkened trunks of fire-scorched spruce trees lie scattered in stark contrast to the snow-covered countryside. This bewildering maze of fallen trees creates a major obstacle through which travel on foot is almost impossible. With spring's arrival, wildflowers, such as fireweed, ragwort, and goldenrod, flourish in the sunlight that now permeates to the charred forest floor, as in Plate 14. Over many years these colourful flowers, as well as willows, Dwarf Birch, and other small bushes, build up the layers of humus. Soon, seedling poplar, birch, pine, and eventually spruce become established between the blackened trunks of the long-dead trees. Drawn to this new source of food, moose, beaver, and other wildlife move into the area. The cycle begins anew.

Nature's simple lines and shapes, rich colours, and textures often combine to form artistically appealing pictures. We are constantly attracted to these images, whether we are flying high in a plane over the devastated landscape of an old burn or just quietly sitting in our canoe, photographing a moose swimming by.

We had been watching shorebirds and simply enjoying the solitude of the marsh, as well as the muted colours of late afternoon. We heard a splash and looked up to see a cow moose pause tentatively at the edge of a small bay nearby. There was a certain abstract quality in the soft, gentle tones, the wavering vertical lines in the water, and the strong, horizontal line of the sedge mat. With a wary eye for us, the moose entered the water, creating yet another dynamic line that adds life and realism to the picture.

PLATE 49   *Dawn in the Camsell Range – December 1987*

PLATE 50   *Moonrise and Hoarfrost – December 1987*

Making like a submarine, canoeists explode from a wave on the upper, wild reaches of the South Nahanni River. Like a great water-slide, this mountain river drops an average of 30 feet every mile, through mile upon mile of boulder-choked Class II and III rapids known appropriately as the Rock Gardens. As with a good fishing yarn, the day's daring deeds take on added lustre and dimension when tired friends gather round the evening camp-fire. To fall asleep listening to the sound of tumbling water through the tent wall and dreaming of tomorrow's promise downriver, round the bend, is a little bit of heaven.

Ah...the delicious, decadent luxury of it all! To bathe in hot water, not just the warm stuff but hot enough to effectively boil your butt should you sit over the wrong vent. We consider a stop at Moore's Hot Springs a reward after long days of pounding through the South Nahanni's icy cold rapids. Somehow, each time we reach this point, half-way between the Little Nahanni and Broken Skull rivers, it is always after a cold, rainy day's paddle. Then the stop seems the more worthwhile. In this picture the solitary bather and the skeletal outline of the fallen tree are enshrouded in rising steam. The image captures, for us, some of the mystery and magic of these warm oases in the wilderness.

PLATE 53   *The Headless Range – March 1987*

PLATE 54   *Being Dropped Off by Twin Otter – September 1987*

The two of us stood in awe, our breath rising as white mist into the cave's cold, enveloping darkness. We had entered this underground world by crawling through a rock-strewn passage in the wall of Death Canyon. With the help of a rope, we had descended a short, subterranean cliff and found ourselves in one of Nature's own treasure houses. Wherever we directed our lights, they ignited objects of dazzling, crystalline beauty. In the warmer zone, near the cave's entrance, hexagonal crystals of sparkling hoarfrost crusted the walls and ceiling. Large and extremely beautiful ice sculptures of the most imaginative and exotic shapes decorated the floor of the great cavern. Transparent stalagmites, with the appearance of inverted tear drops, some as tall as six feet, balanced on the rocky floor, seemingly in defiance of gravity. Two absolutely remarkable curtains of sheer, opalescent ice hung in resplendent folds. This was one of the finest sights we had ever seen.

These unusual and lovely ice formations develop throughout the summer in Igloo Cave when water, percolating through the overlying, warm rock, encounters frigid winter air that has been trapped in the chamber. The heavy cold air cannot escape because the mouth of the cave is higher than much of the main chamber and galleries. The ice, in turn, is carved and scalloped into these marvellous sculptures by the process of sublimation, whereby ice changes directly into water vapour. Man's art would be hard-pressed to surpass this subterranean exhibition of Nature.

From the darkness of a cave we look out across the gently rolling glacial moraine towards the grey limestone wall of Death Canyon. Like moths to a light, we are drawn to these black cave entrances. Nature's passages to the underworld can lead to long, hidden wonders, such as those of Igloo Cave and Grotte Valerie. In the Nahanni Country there are literally hundreds of unexplored caves. Many, perhaps most, lead to nowhere. But, in some, through the ages and in eternal darkness, works of delicate and majestic beauty have been formed. They are there waiting to be discovered. For us, that is the attraction.

PLATE 57 *Spruce Grouse in Spruce Tree – September 1987*

In 1972 Professor Derek Ford of the Geography Department at McMaster University in Hamilton, Ontario, made an astonishing discovery. While checking aerial photographs for signs of limestone outcrops between the South and North Nahanni rivers, he thought he saw something unusual and quite exciting. To be sure, he would have to check it in the field. When he did so later that year, Derek knew he had discovered the first polje in Canada, and not just one but three.

Poljes, a Slav word meaning fields, are common in tropical or warm, temperate, mountainous countries, such as Jamaica, Mexico, and Yugoslavia. However, the Nahanni poljes are, significantly, the only known examples of this karst feature found at such a high latitude anywhere in the world. Here, tucked away in the rugged landscape of the Nahanni Country, a bright green expanse of grass carpets the hard, level floor of Third Polje. The first view of the three Nahanni poljes and the ease of walking across them always come as a pleasant surprise.

Similar to cenotes, poljes originate as fractures in the limestone bedrock. Slowly, through the ages, they deepen and widen by the process of solution to eventually become the largest in the family of closed depressions. Water that enters the poljes drains away through small sinkholes called ponors. One of these can be seen to the right in this picture of Third Polje. During years of heavy rainfall, it is not unusual for water to flow into poljes faster than it drains away. Thus, the lush, green poljes can be transformed into deep lakes literally overnight. Such sporadic flooding inhibits the encroachment of other vegetation. As the water drains away, a fine layer of sediment settles evenly on the polje floor, and the green grass grows once again.

PLATE 58   *Green Grass of Third Polje, Sundog Basin – August 1987*

PLATE 59   *Sluice Box Rapids Below Sunblood Mountain – August 1984*

PLATE 60   *At the Brink, Virginia Falls – August 1984*

PLATE 61   *Thundering Majesty, Virginia Falls – July 1987*

PLATE 62   *Gastropod Fossils Below Virginia Falls – July 1987*

To the native people who journeyed the South Nahanni River long before the coming of the white man, it was known simply as Ná?įlį Cho – big water falling down. What a truly appropriate name for this awesome cataract. In a fury of thunder, mist, and dancing rainbows, the river explodes round a towering, central stack of limestone. It then plummets into the gorge below that is called Painted Canyon or Five-Mile Canyon.

Immediately above the falls is a short but wild and tumultuous stretch of water, the Sluice Box Rapids. Here, the river races and boils through deep and narrow sluices that follow joint lines between large, table-like blocks of limestone. The combined height of these rapids and the falls is about 385 feet – over twice that of Niagara Falls. Virginia Falls is the largest, pristine waterfall of any consequence to be found in North America. It is, in fact, two distinct waterfalls separated by the great rock pinnacle. The high falls at 294 feet and the low falls at 170 feet are receding at about one-third of an inch each year. Painted Canyon was formed by this recession.

Ironically, this magnificent spectacle was named Virginia after the daughter of an influential and wealthy American adventurer who made an exploratory trip to the Nahanni in 1928.

In our picture we wanted to show the power and majesty of the falling water. We kept the image tight. This other photograph shows the ancient snail, *Maclurites*, a gastropod that lived in the warm Ordovician seas that covered the area long ago. Today, below the falls, on the limestone-rubble beach, numerous fossils of this species can be found.

Two Trumpeter Swans and their cygnets cut a wedge-shaped wake across the rain-spattered waters of Yohin Lake. The Trumpeter is the largest, wild waterfowl species in North America. By the early 1900s this elegant bird was dangerously close to extinction because of the active trade in swan skins, unregulated shooting, and a loss of habitat. Swan skins were an article of frontier commerce throughout the nineteenth century, and countless thousands reached the London fur market. Trumpeter Swan quills made quality pens. The soft down was used for powder puffs and the snow-white feathers for adornment. Today these birds of rare and arresting beauty remain uncommon in Canada. With protection, they are making a comeback. Some now raise their young on remote ponds and lakes in the Nahanni Country.

At three in the morning the Moose Ponds and the Itsi Range are touched by the first, soft blush of a June dawn. At this time of year, when sunset is sunrise, the subarctic world literally bursts into bloom. Plants take full advantage of this short respite from the long, dark days of winter. There is a feeling of vibrant energy, as everywhere things are growing, budding, and blossoming. Bees and butterflies flit from flower to flower – flowers that seemed to have appeared only moments before. The floating mats of sedge shed their winter brown as fresh, green spears of growth shoot up through last year's crumpled foliage. On emerging mountain slopes, brilliant splashes of colour – Purple Saxifrage, Arctic Bell Heather, and pink Moss Campion – quickly follow the white of melting snow. It is a time of renewal.

PLATE 65   *Over the Crest, Sunblood Mountain – August 1984*

PLATE 66   *Atop the Nahanni Range – September 1987*

PLATE 67   *Alpine Plants: Purple Saxifrage, Arctic Willow — June 1987*

PLATE 68   *Mount Wilson Reflected in the Moose Ponds – June 1987*

PLATE 69   *The Splits, Lower South Nahanni River – September 1987*

PLATE 70   *Battling Stormy Weather in The Splits – August 1984*

Sunshine on a stormy afternoon highlights the braided pattern of the lower South Nahanni River as it meanders through the notorious Splits. Here, in this broad floodplain at the mouth of the great Nahanni canyons, the wild mountain river finally slows as it nears journey's end. In another 20 miles the river will join with the Liard at distant Nahanni Butte. This ever-changing maze of sinuous waterways can be a nightmare for the river traveller. Currents run every which way. Blind channels open up, only to end in huge driftpiles that can trap the unwary. When storms sweep in, clouds of stinging silt are sent flying from the shingle bars by winds that seem to blow in all directions.

Adventurer R.M. Patterson said it well when writing of his first journey upriver through The Splits in 1927: "[T]he sheltered water had given way to a wide open floodplain strewn with sand-bars, shingle islands, wooded islands, huge driftpiles, and queer, dead-looking forests of snags where uprooted trees had lodged and settled on the river bottom and now, swept clean by ice and floods of all their branches, projected bleakly from the water, their broken tops pointing down river. Through this desolation rushed the Nahanni in, perhaps, two main channels and a maze of smaller ones. From a wooded bank nearby came the thudding lash of 'sweepers' – trees that have been undercut by the floods into the river, but which still cling with their roots to the bank, lashing and beating at the water which drives through their branches. From all sides in this wasteland of the river came the noise of rushing water ... ."[54]

PLATE 71   *Sculpted Beauty, The Sand Blowouts – August 1987*

PLATE 72   *Detail, The Sand Blowouts – August 1987*

From down in The Splits of the South Nahanni River, the Sand Blowouts look like a big, mottled, white patch on the side of a distant hill that lies across from Bluefish Mountain. The native people called it The Wind, a place to be avoided. An old man, Matou, once told a story of a hunter who was stalking a moose near there. He followed the tracks into the Sand Blowouts where suddenly they vanished completely, as though into thin air. He knew the wind had taken the moose.

A hard, three-mile slog from the river through sloughs and dense bush brings the hiker to a desert-like setting of fine-grained sand and stone. Here, it seems hot and parched in stark contrast to the cool, green, surrounding forest. A closer view reveals an intricate, multi-hued landscape of arches, pillars, nubbins, and pedestals of all shapes and sizes. With a little imagination one can see harps, faces, and even a wonderful tropical angelfish carved from sandstone in shades of ivory, mauve, amber, and rose. The ground, which resonates a hollow echo when walked upon, is covered with thousands of colourful sandstone spheres that vary in size and have the appearance of marbles and tennis balls. These delicate sculptures are, by their nature, quite transitory. The soft rock is subject to continuous erosion by the forces of wind and rain.

Our explorations took us beyond the Sand Blowouts into lovely pine woods and valleys, where we found other similar features being formed. One, like a primeval egg, was rising from the rich, deep moss of the forest floor, as in Plate 109.

In this general scene of the Sand Blowouts, we took advantage of the late afternoon sun and the black clouds of an impending storm. The diffused light heightened the sense of drama and allowed for an even exposure. The distant pine adds scale and dimension. In the detailed composition, the same function is served by the small spray of grasses against the ivory sandstone.

PLATE 73   *The South Nahanni Winding Through First Canyon – December 1987*

Winter's chilling grip tightens on the South Nahanni as it winds through First Canyon. This ancient river existed millions of years ago, long before these mountains were thrust up. At that time, it flowed in great, sweeping curves across a broad, flat plain. Forces deep within the Earth caused portions of this plain to be upfolded across the river's course. Like a great knife, the river cut downward as quickly as the land rose up. Today we have the unusual – a meandering, prairie river deeply entrenched in a mountain setting.

The skeleton of a Dall sheep lies entombed in an icy crypt deep within the depths of Grotte Valerie. This animal is but one of over a hundred that have perished in this cave high in the rampart walls of First Canyon. Mountain sheep have often been observed entering caves and other natural rock clefts. Why they do this is not fully understood. Obviously these places offer safe refuge from storms and, perhaps, from predators. George Pellissey, a Mountain Indian, tells of ewes and young lambs entering caves to avoid ambush by eagles. For whatever reason, Grotte Valerie has been a death trap for over 2,000 years.

Singularly or in small groups, most of the animals that died had wandered 1,000 feet back to the blind passage known as The Gallery of the Dead Sheep. A steeply inclined ice-slide marks the entrance to this fateful gallery. Once below the miniature, underground glacier, the sheep became trapped. Death resulted from disorientation, cold, and lack of food. Rodents entered the chamber to eat the carcasses, disturbing and jumbling the bones. Some of these scavengers themselves expired, including the porcupine that rests behind the large ram skull photographed in Plate 11.

We illuminated this picture to draw attention first to the skeleton and then to the deadly ice-slide, decorated with candle-like stalagmites.

PLATE 75   *The Thunderdome and Hole-in-the-Wall Lake – September 1987*

PLATE 76   *Breaking Camp Along the Liard River – September 1987*

The majestic Thunderdome looms above Hole-in-the-Wall Lake in this brilliant fall scene. The rust red hues of Dwarf Birch, the yellow gold of Trembling Aspen, and the pale green of willow spill down the mountain slopes. Dwarf Birch, whose lovely autumn colours paint much of the northern landscape, is a tenacious, little shrub that seldom exceeds six feet in height. It is a plant that is easy to love and hate at the same time. We have stood in awe as it flaunted its fiery September tones, as in Plates 4 and 25, and have watched with pleasure as snowy ptarmigan nibbled its buds in winter. But, oh, how we have cursed it when hiking for miles through its tangled, entrapping mat. We have come to know and respect it by its other appropriate name – shin tangle.

This was one of those fall mornings you dream of – still, calm, not a cloud in the sky, a perfect day for paddling. We drifted with the current, saw a couple of Sandhill Cranes on a gravel bar, and spotted a Black bear in the white and gold of the aspen. A few hours later, as it is wont to do in the North, an autumnal gale arose, and we were battling our way through two-foot waves.

135

PLATE 77   *Dall Sheep Crossing Scree Slope – August 1987*

PLATE 78   *Crash Canyon and Crash Lake – August 1987*

PLATE 79   *Hidden Lake, The Nahanni Plateau — August 1987*

PLATE 80   *Blossoms of the Arctic Bell Heather – June 1987*

PLATE 81   *The Prairie Creek Canyon – August 1984*

PLATE 82   *The Gate and Pulpit Rock – July 1987*

Golden sunlight spills into Prairie Creek Canyon, illuminating the high cliffs along this clear, cold creek that winds its way down through the Nahanni Plateau. Tributary canyons of the South Nahanni River, such as Prairie Creek and Lafferty Creek, are always a joy to go hiking in. There are huge, water-worn boulders to scramble over and around, cliffs honeycombed with caves to explore, and many handy pools for a cooling dip on a hot summer's day, as in Plate 89. Along Prairie Creek, in quiet eddies below boulders and in deep, dark pools by the canyon walls, lurk succulent Arctic grayling and Dolly Varden. A line dropped here will likely mean fresh fish sizzling over the evening camp-fire.

Dwarfed by the towering, 250-foot spire of Pulpit Rock, a canoe passes through The Gate in Third Canyon. Early explorers, tracking and poling up the South Nahanni River, named the three great canyons they encountered First, Second, and Third respectively. In places, these awesome gashes are almost a mile in depth. Together they have a combined length of 47 miles. This canyon system was once much more extensive. The South Nahanni River is slowly straightening as it becomes more deeply entrenched. As a result, large, abandoned meanders are left hanging high and dry.

The Gate is the most recent example of this process. Thousands of years ago, water began to trickle through a vertical crack in the neck of a hairpin turn. Over time this crack developed into a cavern through which the water thundered. Eventually, the unstable roof collapsed. The full volume of the river now flowed through this new route by way of The Gate. The river was shortened by two miles. Pulpit Rock is a residual fragment of the old cave wall, preserved between the modern channel and an older branch.

PLATE 83   *South Nahanni River Near Hell Roaring Creek – August 1984*

PLATE 84   *The Bald Eagle, Beauty and Power in Motion – July 1987*

PLATE 85   *Mud Cracks and Caribou Tracks – August 1987*

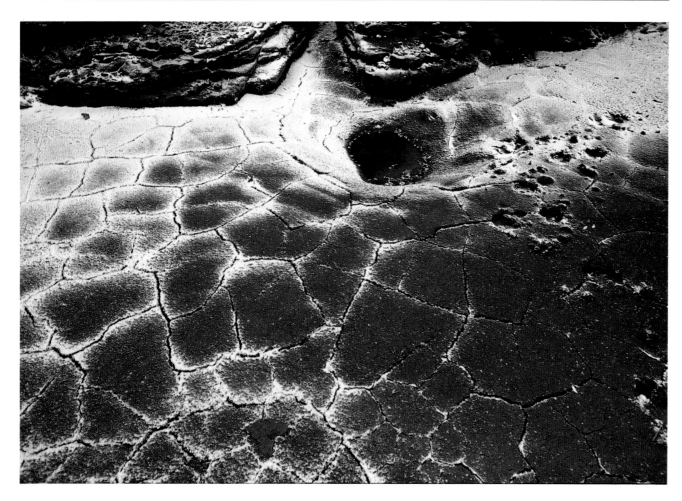

Common visual elements abound in much of what we see in the natural world. Similarities exist in these two photographs, despite the tremendous difference in the size of the subjects. The shapes of dry mud etched by snowy cracks on the bottom of a small solution sinkhole resemble the immense flows of ice on the inky-blue waters of the great Mackenzie River.

The picture above covers an area of roughly ten feet by seven. It was taken high on the dry limestone surface of the Nahanni Plateau. A caribou, seeking water, entered this sinkhole from the upper right. The animal paused to drink from the leaf-rimmed pool, all that remains of the larger pond that has drained away. These tracks add perspective and interest to a picture that is otherwise a puzzle.

In the opposite image, ice-flows move down the Mackenzie below Gros Cap at the confluence of the Liard River. These are shapes on a grand scale, where even a small flow can be the size of a football field. During freeze-up, ice grinds to a halt at a bottleneck below Fort Simpson. Soon, winter's stillness will settle over the river.

PLATE 86 *Ice-flows on the Mackenzie River – December 1987*

Under stormy winter clouds, the distant wall of the Nahanni Range rises above the Great Slave Plain of the Mackenzie Lowlands. Marching in a solid line across the horizon, these peaks are the outriders, sentinels of the vast mountain kingdom that lies beyond. The nearly flat, low-lying terrain, through which the frozen Liard River winds is covered by muskeg and numerous, small, shallow lakes. The silt clay soils support forests of birch, poplar, and spruce in mixed and pure stands. Here, in this wild country, Moose and Wood bison are very much at home.

Two massive bull bison move in unison along the soft, silty bank of The Splits on the lower South Nahanni River. These wild, free-ranging Wood bison are part of a herd that has been successfully re-established in the Liard Valley. By the 1930s, Wood bison were believed to be extinct, the surviving few having been inadvertently cross-bred with the Plains bison. In 1957 a small, isolated, nearly pure herd of 200 animals was discovered in a remote corner of Canada's Wood Buffalo National Park. Efforts to protect and propagate these bison have met with success. Hopefully, in the near future these animals will be removed from the Endangered Species List.

PLATE 91   *Confluence of the Flat and Caribou Rivers – September 1987*

They stare out at us from the past, young faces in old, brown photographs. There was hope there, hope and dreams of finding the mother lode, of seeing the glint of yellow gold in the bottom of a pan. We see them with their dogs, their packs, and their sleds. We see them dipping a pan along a gravel bar or poling a scow. We see them up there on the tributaries of the Flat River, standing by a log cabin or manning a sluice box – all of them searching, seeking that elusive, golden glint. We know their names, a few at least... Willie and Frank McLeod, Yukon Fisher, Martin Jorgensen, Poole Field, Diamond C, Albert Faille, Bill Powers, Jonas Lafferty, Bill Epler, Charles Yohin, Gus Kraus, Dick Turner. Others are forgotten faces from another time, another age.

Few found their dreams in that wild country, up the South Nahanni and Flat rivers. Some, an unusual number, died mysteriously to become part of the Nahanni legend. All of them, at one time or another, found their way up the Flat River seen here as autumn's golden hues touch the gravel bars at the mouth of the Caribou. Some poled and lined their way up the South Nahanni River through Painted Canyon where the bluffs and cliffs of Sunblood limestone have weathered to a golden yellow.

An Indian named Little Nahanni brought rich, gold-bearing quartz into Fort Liard around 1900. From then on, there were persistent rumours of placer gold up in the Nahanni Country. Many men embarked on what was to be a futile search, for little gold was ever found.

PLATE 92   *Canoeing Through Painted Canyon – August 1984*

PLATE 93   *Entering Deadmen Valley From Second Canyon – August 1984*

PLATE 94   *Ridge-walking in the Clouds, The Ram Plateau – August 1987*

A flight of geese takes wing against a dark, ominous sky as canoeists enter Deadmen Valley. Here, in this strikingly beautiful valley just beyond the last, precipitous cliffs of Second Canyon, the gruesome stories got their start.

On the gravel bank at the mouth of Headless Creek, the skeletal bodies of Willie and Frank McLeod were found in 1908. Or was it 1907? Whenever.... There are as many versions of this tale as there are storytellers. Did the brothers discover a fabulous gold mine, its location now long lost? Were they killed by a fierce band of mythical mountain Indians and their white chieftess? Or by the evil spirits said to haunt "that mysterious land of doom and disaster?"[55] Did they die at the hand of a gold-crazed partner named Weir? Was Weir, or was it Ware, even with them? Did Charlie McLeod, another brother, track Weir down years later, and did Weir shoot himself atop a burning haystack? Were the McLeods simply greedy men, ill prepared for the rigours of this wild land? Or were they expert hunters, completely at home in the wilderness? Was their gear lost in a boating accident, and did they then lie down and starve to death, together side by side? For that matter, were they lying down, sitting up, or tied to a tree when discovered? And who found them – their brother Charlie, Poole Field, the Mounties? Were they headless, and, if they were, where did the skulls go? Did those nasty goblins get them, or did scavengers such as bears and wolverines?

Who really knows; does it really matter? Like all the other stories, such as that of Martin Jorgensen who turned up a few years later as a charred, headless skeleton or that of John O'Brien who froze to death, nugget hard, kneeling by his fire atop the Twisted Mountain, they are great yarns to be told and retold by the flickering light of camp-fires. The Nahanni, with its stories, legends, and mystery, has become part of the vernacular Canadian folklore.

Many Nahanni legends have their roots in the unfortunate deaths of people who were unprepared for the harshness of the land and the vagaries of the weather. At any time, with little forewarning, the weather can become the major factor governing human survival. For most of the year, the boundary between two great air masses – the cool, dry Arctic air and the warm, moist Pacific air – lies directly over the Nahanni Country. Extremely unstable and unpredictable weather is the result, as these air masses continually vie for position. Here, we hike along a cloud-enshrouded ledge high above the Ram Canyons on what will soon be a sunny day.

PLATE 95   *Gypsy Mushroom in Reindeer Moss – September 1987*

PLATE 96   *The Ram River and the North Nahanni Plateau – December 1987*

PLATE 97   *A Glacier's Icy Tongue – July 1987*

PLATE 98   *Canoeing Towards the Ragged Range – August 1984*

A lone sentinel, a pinnacle of sandstone carved by unnumbered centuries of wind, rain, and frost, stands guard on a ridge of the Tlogotsho Range overlooking Ram Creek. The table-like mountain in the distance beyond the creek is part of this range. Its flat summit is typical of all the mountains in the area, colloquially known as the Tlogotsho Plateau. Tlogotsho means big prairie, an apt description for this treeless tundra of lichens, mosses, sedges, grasses, and clusters of tiny alpine flowers. It is ideal habitat for Dall sheep, which are found here in abundance. Yet, it is also a world marked by cold and dampness. The continual freezing and thawing of the water-saturated soil heaves rocks out of the ground, dropping them into some of the most remarkable, polygonal patterns we have ever seen.

We live in a three-dimensional world, which is reduced to a flat, two-dimensional image when photographed. When looking at pictures of the natural world, where no familiar reference points exist, the viewer is often left in a quandary as to the size of objects. How high is the waterfall? How deep is the canyon? Or, as in the facing picture, how big is the rock pinnacle? A person, animal, or some vegetation included in the composition can often help. The Arctic ground squirrel is not very big. We gain this perspective from the tall grasses that surround the diminutive animal. Here, the squirrel enjoys the warm, morning sunshine outside one of several entrances to its burrow.

PLATE 101 *Skiing Towards the Gap, Little Doctor Lake – April 1987*

PLATE 102 *The Ram Plateau – August 1987*

The growth of the Wisconsin-Laurentide ice-sheet, beginning some 25,000 years ago, was the last major advance of the Great Ice Age. The immense, grinding weight of this glacial mass moving slowly westward was blocked by the imposing wall of the Nahanni Range. In a few places the ice managed to penetrate this barrier, gouging out deep, cliff-bound passes through the mountains. Today, roughly 10,000 years after the ice retreated, we see the results of this breach at such points as Cli and Little Doctor lakes.

Little Doctor Lake, seen here on a winter's day, was named after a local medicine man. The natives also know this very beautiful lake as Túeku, choppy water, because strong winds often funnel through the Gap, whipping up large waves.

On another occasion the weather was sunny and cold as we skied across the lake. For some time we heard the wind moaning through the lofty crags, high overhead. Down where we were, there was not even a breath. Suddenly, gale-force winds almost flattened us. We were in a chinook! Dry air flowing across the mountains to the west is compressed and heated as it swiftly descends the eastern slopes. The wind, screaming through the Gap, was so warm that powder snow turned almost instantly to slush. Very quickly, puddles of water formed, and skiing with heavy packs became an arduous chore.

A day's hike beyond the Gap and across the Tetcela River is the spectacular Ram River country with its deep canyons, lofty palisades, sculpted terraces, and broad plateaus. In character, the land is more reminiscent of the American Southwest; it is not something one expects to find in the remote, subarctic wilderness.

PLATE 103 *Mountain Goat on Cliff Face – August 1984*

A Mountain goat peers back from its vantage point high on a precipitous cliff in the Ragged Range. We have often watched these sure-footed creatures cavorting about in their rugged, mountain domain, following trails along narrow ledges that drop off to nowhere and bounding in great leaps from one rocky outcrop to another. Its scientific name (*Oreamnos* from the Greek "mountain lamb") and its common name confusingly imply that this animal is closely related to sheep and goats. It belongs, in fact, to a small group of Mountain antelopes. Here, we show the animal in its environment, a vertical world of rock and space.

On a sunny day, hikers cross the verdant Fairy Meadow in the Cirque of the Unclimbables. Surrounding this sublime ice-carved, mountain amphitheatre are sheer cliffs that challenge mountaineers from around the world. The Ragged Range has superb, alpine scenery with a jumble of razor-sharp peaks, ice-fields, glaciers, azure lakes, and deep valleys. These mountains are built of quartz monzonite, a highly resistant variety of granite. Millions of years ago this rock was injected into the Earth's crust from the underlying mantle as a mass of molten magma.

PLATE 107   *Winter in the Canyon Ranges – December 1987*

APPENDIX

PAT AND ROSEMARIE KEOUGH

"A bosom friend [is]...a really kindred spirit to whom I can confide my inmost soul," declared Canada's beloved Anne of Green Gables in that classic tale. Had she lived today, Anne would have undoubtedly applied this epithet to the Keoughs.

Since 1984, when they first met on a canoe expedition in the Nahanni wilderness, Pat and Rosemarie Keough have been quite inseparable. Something clicked up there, in that wild country, on those churning white waters. Perhaps it was a mutual recognition: each loves and appreciates the natural world. Perhaps it was a mutual objective: each has a driving determination to excel at whatever they do. They are a couple, in the truest sense of the word. They think alike, they work side by side, and they are each other's best friend.

Before meeting, their keen, individual interests in wildlife, natural beauty, and other cultures had frequently taken Pat and Rosemarie to far-off corners of the world. Photography was a consuming and stimulating hobby for both, whose professional careers lay in other fields. Once married, they desired a future that would give them the opportunity to work closely together. What better way than to combine some of their abiding passions – photography, adventure, travel, and conservation – in a rewarding, satisfying career.

Travel features – on hitherto little known areas of the Ottawa Valley, their home; the Nahanni Country, where they met; and the jungles of the Far East, where they spent their honeymoon – began to appear in national newspapers. Soon their work was profiled on radio and television shows across Canada. Their photography was included in several major books.

From the beginning, Rosemarie and Pat had a goal to create a series of very high quality, informative, and beautiful books. These books would feature their photography and writing while showcasing unique regions of Canada and the world.

Through great effort and determination, *The Ottawa Valley Portfolio* was published by their aptly named company, Nahanni Productions, in 1986. This coffee-table book was the first to be devoted entirely to their own work. Within a few months it became a bestseller, a phenomenal success.

The Keoughs had another dream, to return to the wild grandeur of the Nahanni Country, the chosen subject for Volume 2 of the portfolio series. The success of the first book made *The Nahanni Portfolio* a reality. Like its predecessor, it, too, has the Keough stamp of quality. The photographs are splendid; the writing is vivid; the design and production speak of excellence.

To create these breathtaking images meant travelling through rugged, wild country, in canoe, bush plane, and helicopter and on foot, snowshoes, and skis. It meant surviving all kinds of weather: rain, wind, sun, and snow. It meant being alone, together, for months at a time, without another soul within hundreds of miles. But for all of that, the Keoughs are comfortable in the wilderness and view the experience as a marvellous and memorable adventure.

The Keoughs are nature photographers whose artistic perception and sense of composition show infinite patience and attention to the minutest detail. It is not unusual for them to wait hours or even days for just the right lighting, cloud formation, or reflection to capture the quintessential quality they desire. It is obvious that they understand the character and significance of their subject matter.

Rosemarie and Pat have an eye for that fleeting moment of beauty. Juxtaposed with their magnificent landscapes are wildlife pictures that are more than simple portraits. There is a distinct tension, a feeling of expectation evident in their images of birds and animals: a Bald Eagle swooping low across a slate grey sky; a Mountain goat pausing tentatively on a sheer cliff face.

Pat and Rosemarie never indicate who took which photograph. And if you were to ask, you still wouldn't know. The Keoughs do not remember, and it does not matter to them. As a team, they will often mutually compose an image. When both are satisfied, they trip the shutter. Working together this way means that individual egos have to be brushed aside. The right picture must take precedence over feelings.

The Keoughs work in similar fashion when writing. They write and rewrite until both are happy with the result. In addition to demonstrating a sensibility to each other's tastes, Pat and Rosemarie thoroughly research their subject. Their books are replete with interesting historical material and snippets of information not known to the average person.

Photography and writing are tools used by the Keoughs to present a key message: the beauty and intricacy of the natural world must be preserved. So park benches, city streets, shopping malls, and crowds of people cannot be found in the Keoughs' books.

There are photographers who like to depict the human race. The Keoughs' approach, to depict nature, is a different way of looking at the world. Through such portraiture, Rosemarie and Pat are virtually saying, "Let Nature have these pages and let Man take a back seat."

No one can argue that the natural world dominates the vision of Pat and Rosemarie. Certainly, *The Ottawa Valley Portfolio* and *The Nahanni Portfolio* are splendid portrayals of the authors' vision. The reader can expect to see more of the same splendour in the third volume of the portfolio series, which will celebrate the natural wonder of the Niagara Escarpment.

Heather Lang-Runtz

Pat and Rosemarie by Cabin, Little Doctor Lake
Pat With Firewood, After Photographing Birds
Rosemarie Climbing to Photograph Dall Sheep
Pat and Rosemarie by Camp-fire During August Blizzard

INDEX TO THE COLOUR PLATES

Arctic Tern

PLATE 108 *After the Rain, Camp-site Above The Splits – August 1987*

ANNOTATED LIST OF PLACE NAMES

Listed below are official names of some of the places and features of the Nahanni Country, followed by anecdotes recalled by local elders. Where available, the Dene name is given along with a translation.

Blackstone River. Tthet'eah – Burned little stones.

Clearwater Creek – Origin unknown. Albert Faille called it Murder Creek in reference to Martin Jorgensen's death.

Deadmen Valley – Named by Poole Field around 1907 upon finding the headless skeletons of Frank and Willie McLeod near the bank of the South Nahanni River in this valley. **Dahtaehtth'į** – Barren, wide-open area along the bank of the river.

Direction Mountain – Bush pilot Wop May is believed to have coined this name in the 1930s for the distinctive peak at the confluence of the South Nahanni and Flat rivers. This peak was used as a landmark to the supposed gold fields of the Flat River.

First Canyon – The first of three canyons named in succession by Poole Field when on a journey up the South Nahanni River. **Ala Tthe Zhihgonįá** – Hole going right through the first rock.

Flat River – Origin unknown. **Tu Negaa Dehe** – White water boiling river.

Fort Liard – Founded by the North West Company in 1805 as Fort aux Liards. Liard, an old French word, refers to the grey-green leaves of the poplar tree, which is numerous in the area. **Echaot'įne Kǫ́ę́** – Community of the people who are different.

Fort Simpson – Fort of the Forks was established in 1804 by the North West Company at the confluence of the Mackenzie and Liard rivers. In 1821 the Forks became a Hudson's Bay Company post and was later renamed Fort Simpson in honour of Sir George Simpson, head of the Northern Department of the company. **Łíidlį Kǫ́ę́** – Community where the two rivers meet.

The Gate – Believed to have been named by Poole Field to describe the tight constriction of the South Nahanni River by surrounding cliffs. **Tthe Eht'ahįah** – Rocks are bound, knitted, close together.

Hell's Gate – Describes a particularly treacherous part of the South Nahanni River where two enormous whirlpools meet with large standing waves. Previously called Rapid-That-Runs-Both-Ways, as named by R.M. Patterson, and also Figure-of-Eight Rapids, as named by Albert Faille. **Tuʔat'ą́ą́nalį** – Water flowing backward in a curve.

Kraus Hot Springs – The sulphur thermal pools at the edge of the South Nahanni River below First Canyon, where Gus and Mary Kraus lived. **Tu Łetsęę** – Smelly water.

Lafferty Creek – A boulder-strewn creek named after Jonas Lafferty, who was among a party of prospectors staking claims along the creek around 1922. **Tthe Cho Dehe** – Big rock river.

Liard River – Earlier known as River of the Mountains. See Fort Liard. **Naechagáh** – River that boils again and again.

Little Doctor Lake – A large and often windy lake, named by Dr. Truesdell of Fort Simpson after a short and respected medicine man, the grandfather of John Tetso. **Túeka** – Choppy water.

Mackenzie River – The tenth longest river in the world, named by John Franklin after Alexander Mackenzie, the first white man to explore the entire length of the river. **Dehcho** – The grand river.

May Creek – Named after May Lafferty, an in-law of Poole Field, who went missing in 1921 nearby, never to be seen again. **Ts'élįa Ts'éʔetłah Dehe** – A little-girl-got-lost creek.

McLeod Creek – Named by Jack Stanier and Bill Clark in 1935 where they found old gold workings, which they believed were those of the ill-fated McLeod brothers. They later agreed that the relics found by Gus Kraus on nearby Bennett Creek more likely belonged to the McLeods.

Mount Harrison Smith – Named in 1937 by Harry Snyder, an American big game specimen collector, after a business associate.

Nahanni Butte – Name of the dome-shaped mountain and the community located at its base at the mouth of the South Nahanni River. Originally an independent trading post called South Nahanni up to the late 1930s, its name was changed to Nahanni Butte by Gus Kraus and Jack LaFlair to avoid further confusion with the post called North Nahanni at the mouth of the North Nahanni River. **Tthenago** – Rock bends down (into the lowlands). **Tsa Kǫ́ę́** – Beaver lodge.

North Nahanni River – Known as Rocky Mountain River to the early white traders. **Shíh Tah Nilį Dehe** – Flowing-through-the-mountains river. **Mbehzęah** – Cut with a knife (in reference to the tight canyons).

Prairie Creek – Name refers to the extensive tundra known as the Caribou Flats at the headwaters. **Kádadaatłah Dehe** – River of the clearing formed by forest fire. **Tł'o Dehe** – Grass river.

Pulpit Rock – A rock formation resembling a church pulpit at the downstream end of The Gate. Named Pulpit Rock by R. M. Patterson and previously known to Gus Kraus as the Gate-post.

Rabbitkettle Tufa Mound – A large conical mound of soft crystalline rock formed by a warm spring that wells up through the mound. **Gah Tth'a** – Rabbit pot (in reference to a legend that long ago the spring waters were so hot that people cooked rabbits in it).

Sand Blowouts – Exotic sandstone sculptures carved by wind and rain. Called the Devil's Kitchen by Gus and Mary Kraus.

Nįhts'i Thekǫ – The wind sits in a bowl. **Nįhts'i Enda** – Living wind.

Seaplane Lake – Named by bush pilot H.A. Doc Oakes, who in 1928 was the first pilot to land on the Flat River watershed. Also known locally as Landing Lake.

South Nahanni River – Named the Nahany River by W. F. Wentzel around 1805 after the *Nahany* Indians. **Nahʔąa Dehe** – River of the Nahʔąa People. Gus and Mary Kraus give the following translation, Setting Sun River, which refers to the west-east orientation of the river.

The Splits – The lower section of the South Nahanni River that is braided to the extreme. **Ndu Tah** – Among the islands.

Sunblood Mountain – The distinctive mountain above Virginia Falls that appears red in the sunlight. Named by George Dalziel, a bush pilot and trapper.

Tlogotsho Range – A flat-topped range of barren mountains colloquially called the Tlogotsho Plateau, known for an abundance of Dall sheep. **Tł'o K'é Gocho** – Big Place of Grass.

The Twisted Mountain – Previously called O'Brien Mountain after a trapper who froze to death atop its long, sloping wall. The official and descriptive name was coined by a government geologist exploring the oil and coal potential of the area in 1949. **Kánajoh** – Something big pushing up, emerging.

Vera Creek – Named in 1954 after Vera Turner by a topographic survey party who were offered warm, northern hospitality by Dick and Vera Turner.

Virginia Falls – Named by Fenley Hunter after his daughter Virginia. Hunter was an American businessman and adventurer, who in 1928 made an exploratory trip up the South Nahanni River to the falls. He subsequently divorced his wife and apparently saw very little of his daughter after. **Náʔįlį Cho** – Big water falling down.

Yohin Lake – Named after Charles Yohin and his father, well-known and respected Dene who trapped in that area. Also locally known as Jackfish Lake because on this lake the people of Nahanni Butte winter fish for Jackfish (pike). **Chi Tú** – Duck lake.

PLATE 109 *Deep in the Forest, A New Sand Blowout Emerges – August 1987*

FOOTNOTES

1. 'Dene' is an Athapaskan word that means 'the people.' The term Dene refers collectively to the native people of the Northwest Territories and includes the Slavey, Dogrib, Hareskin, Loucheux, and Chipewyan bands.

2, 12. Wendell E. White, *Birth of Nahanni "Nahande Beguli": A Local History of the People of Nahanni Butte* (Nahanni Butte, 1984), p.5.

3, 13. Governor George Simpson's letter of January 2, 1823, to A. R. McLeod cited in R. M. Patterson, "The Nahany Lands," in *The Beaver*, Summer 1961, p.40.

4. The geological history of the Nahanni Country, written by Pat and Rosemarie Keough, is based primarily on the excellent work and detailed research of Professor Derek Ford, Department of Geology, McMaster University, Hamilton, Ontario.

5. Derek C. Ford, "The Extraordinary Landscape of South Nahanni," in *Canadian Geographic Journal*, Volume 94, No. 1, 1977, p.61.

6. Charles Yohin cited in Wendell E. White, *Birth of Nahanni "Nahande Beguli": A Local History of the People of Nahanni Butte* (Nahanni Butte, 1984), p.23.

7. Baptiste Cazon cited in Lanny Cooke and Camille Piche, OMI, *Łíídlį Kǫ́ę́: Two Rivers of Faith – Fort Simpson, Denendeh* (Yellowknife: Native Communications Society of the Western N.W.T., n.d.), p.17.

8. Charles Camsell, *Son of the North* (Toronto: Ryerson Press, 1954), p.6.

9. Paraphrased Fragment of Journal by Willard Ferdinand Wentzel at Grand River Near McKenzie's River 1805 & 1806. MG19/El. [Ottawa: Public Archives of Canada]. Cited in Shepard Krech III, *The Subarctic Fur Trade: Native Social and Economic Adaptations* (Vancouver: University of British Columbia Press, 1984), p.107.

10. Journal of John Thompson, Esq., McKenzie River, Winter 1800-1801. [Montreal: McGill University Libraries]. Cited ibid., p.106.

11. W. F. Wentzel's letter to Mr. Roderick McKenzie, McKenzie River, April 30, 1811, cited in *Les Bourgeois de la Compagnie du Nord-Ouest*, volume 1, ed. L. R. Masson (New York: Antiquarian Press, 1889), pp. 106-7.

14. John M. McLeod cited in R. M. Patterson, "The Nahany Lands," in *The Beaver*, Summer 1961, p.44.

15. Hudson's Bay Company Journal, Fort Simpson 1824 Hudson's Bay Company Archives B.200/a/4,fo.10d].

16. Robert Campbell cited in C. Parnell, "Campbell of the Yukon," in *The Beaver*, June 1942, p.5.

17. Bishop Grandin cited in Lanny Cooke and Camille Piche, OMI, *Łíídlį Kǫ́ę́: Two Rivers of Faith – Fort Simpson, Denendeh* (Yellowknife: Native Communications Society of the Western N.W.T., n.d.), p.16.

18. Stanley Isaiah cited ibid., p.11.

19. Kerry M. Abel, "The South Nahanni River Region, Northwest Territories (1820-1972): Patterns of Socio-Economic Transition in the Canadian North," (Master's thesis, University of Manitoba, Winnipeg, 1980), p.45.

20. Bishop Grandin cited in Lanny Cooke and Camille Piche, OMI, *Łíídlį Kǫ́ę́: Two Rivers of Faith – Fort Simpson, Denendeh* (Yellowknife: Native Communications Society of the Western N.W.T., n.d.), p.23.

21. Rev. Father S. Lesage, *Sacred Heart Mission, Fort Simpson, N.W.T., 1858-1958* (Fort Simpson; Oblates, 1959), p.14.

22. ibid., p.15.

23. ibid., p.15.

24. *Klondike Nugget*, July 5, 1899, cited in Pierre Berton, *Klondike* (Toronto: McClelland and Stewart, 1972), pp.218-9.

25. Pierre Berton, *The Mysterious North* (New York: Alfred A. Knopf, 1956), p.69.

26, 52. Philip H. Godsell's manuscript, "The Curse of Dead Man's Valley," p.6 [Glenbow-Alberta Institute, Calgary, Alberta].

27. Poole Field's letter to J. Moran, dated Nahanni, July 17, 1939, p.19 [Glenbow-Alberta Institute, Calgary, Alberta].

28. Dick Turner, *Nahanni* (Surrey: Hancock House, 1975), pp.168-9.

29. *The Edmonton Journal*, March 16, 1929, cited in Kerry M. Abel, "The South Nahanni River Region, Northwest Territories (1820-1972): Patterns of Socio-Economic Transition in the Canadian North," (Master's thesis, University of Manitoba, Winnipeg, 1980), p.149.

30. R.M. Patterson, *The Dangerous River* (London: George Allen and Unwin Ltd., 1954), p.34.

31. William Weintraub, "The Obsession of Albert Faille" (no reference, n.d.), p.32.

32. Fred Sibbeston, personal interview, December 1987.

33. Cited in Jean Morisset and Rose Marie Pelletier, *Ted Trindell: Metis Witness to the North* (Vancouver: Tillacum Library, 1986), p.25.

34. ibid., back cover.

35. Charles Camsell, *Son of the North* (Toronto: Ryerson Press, 1954), p.12.

36. Canada, Department of Mines, *Summary Report*, 1920, Part B, p.58B. Cited in Rene Fumoleau, *As Long As This Land Shall Last* (Toronto: McClelland and Stewart Limited, 1973), p.153.

37. Public Archives Canada, RG10, BC, file 336,877, Conroy to Scott, 6 February 1920. Cited ibid., p.158.

38. Ibid., McLean to Conroy, 13 May 1921., Cited ibid., p.163.

39. Rene Fumoleau, *As Long As This Land Shall Last* (Toronto: McClelland and Stewart Limited, 1973), p.164.

40. IBNWTA, Transcript of Ted Trindell's narrative, 3 January 1973. Cited ibid., p.175.

41. Fred Sibbeston, personal interview, December 1987.

42. Bill Lafferty, personal interview, December 1987.

43. Philip H. Godsell, *Arctic Trader* (New York: G.P. Putnam's Sons, 1934), pp.304-5. Cited in Rene Fumoleau, *As Long As This Land Shall Last* (Toronto: McClelland and Stewart Limited, 1973), p.265.

44. Helge Ingstad, *The Land of Feast and Famine* (New York: Alfred A. Knopf, 1933), pp.150-2. Cited ibid., p.357.

45. R.M. Patterson, "River of Deadmen's Valley," in *The Beaver*, June 1947, p.13.

46. Dick Turner, *Wings of the North* (Surrey: Hancock House Publishers Ltd., 1980), p.43.

47. Ron Sprang, personal interview, October 1987.

48. Mansell Patterson, personal interview, December 1987.

49. Pete Cowie, personal interview, December 1987.

50. Ibid.

51. R.M. Patterson, *The Dangerous River* (London: George Allen and Unwin Ltd., 1954), p.8.

53. John Murray, "Nahanni National Park: Deadmen Valley Log Book", Entry of August 9, 1982.

54. R.M. Patterson, *The Dangerous River* (London: George Allen and Unwin Ltd., 1954) p.36.

55. Philip H. Godsell's manuscript, "The Curse of Dead Man's Valley," p.22 [Glenbow-Alberta Institute, Calgary, Alberta].

A GLIMPSE OF HISTORY – PICTURE CREDITS

Hoary Marmot

SELECTED REFERENCES

*Abel, Kerry M. "The South Nahanni River Region, Northwest Territories (1820-1972): Patterns of Socio-Economic Transition in the Canadian North." Master's thesis, University of Manitoba, Winnipeg, 1980.

Addison, W.E., and Addison, W.D. *Nahanni National Park Historical Resources Inventory: A Preliminary Chronology.* Ottawa: Environment Canada – Parks, 1976.

Addison, W.E., and Addison, W.D. *Nahanni National Park Historical Resources Inventory: Vol. 1, Interviews with R. M. Patterson and Willy McLeod. Vol. 2, Interview with Gus Kraus. Vol. 3, Interviews of Bill Clark and Albert Faille.* Ottawa: Environment Canada – Parks, 1975-76.

Berger, Thomas R. *Northern Frontier, Northern Homeland: The Report of the Mackenzie Valley Pipeline Inquiry, Vol. 1.* Toronto: James Lorimer & Co., 1977.

Boudreau, Norman J. *The Athapaskans: Strangers of the North.* Ottawa: National Museum of Man, 1974.

**Brook, George A., and Ford, Derek C. *The Karstlands of the South Nahanni Region, Mackenzie Mountains, N.W.T.* Ottawa: Environment Canada – Parks, 1976.

Camsell, Charles. *Son of the North.* Toronto: Ryerson Press, 1954.

Churcher, C.S. Palaeozoological Study of the Dead Dall Sheep in Grotto Valerie, Nahanni National Park. Ottawa: Environment Canada – Parks, 1974.

Ellis, Frank H. *Canada's Flying Heritage.* Toronto: University of Toronto Press, 1954.

Fiennes, Ranulph. *The Headless Valley.* London: Hodder and Stoughton, 1973.

**Ford, Derek C. *Final Report Upon Cavern and Allied Researches in the First Canyon Area, South Nahanni River, N.W.T.* Ottawa: Environment Canada – Parks, 1971.

**Ford, Derek C. *Final Report on the Geomorphology of South Nahanni National Park, N.W.T.* Ottawa: Environment Canada – Parks, 1974.

**Ford, D.C., and Quinlan, J.F. *Theme and Resource Inventory Study of the Karst Regions of Canada.* Ottawa: Environment Canada – Parks, 1973.

Frison-Roche, Roger. *Nahanni.* Grenoble: B. Arthaud, 1969.

Fumoleau, Rene. *As Long as This Land Shall Last.* Toronto: McClelland and Stewart Limited, 1973.

Fumoleau, Rene. *Denendeh: A Dene Celebration.* Yellowknife: The Dene Nation, 1984.

Gimbarzevsky, P., Peaker, J.P., Addison, P., and Talbot, S. *Nahanni National Park, Northwest Territories: Integrated Survey of Biophysical Resources, Volumes 1, 2, 3.* Ottawa: Environment Canada – Parks, 1979.

Hall, Ed. *A Way of Life.* Yellowknife: Government of the Northwest Territories, Department of Renewable Resources, 1986.

Henry, Walter, and the Canadian Bush Pilot Book Project. *Uncharted Skies: Canadian Bush Pilot Stories.* Edmonton: Reidmore Books, n.d.

Krech III., Shepard, ed. *The Subarctic Fur Trade: Native Social and Economic Adaptations.* Vancouver: University of British Columbia Press, 1984.

Lesage, Rev. Father S. *Sacred Heart Mission, Fort Simpson, N.W.T., 1858-1958.* Fort Simpson: Oblates, 1959.

McCormick, Kevin J., and Shandruk, Len J. *A Survey of Trumpeter Swans and Their Habitat in Southern Mackenzie District, Northwest Territories, 1986.* Yellowknife: Canadian Wildlife Service, 1987.

Moore, Joanne Ronan. *Nahanni Trailhead.* Ottawa: Deneau and Greenberg Publishers Ltd., 1980.

Morice, A.G. *The Great Dene Race.* Vienna: Administration of "Anthropos," The Press of the Mechitharistes, 1910.

Morisset, Jean, and Pelletier, Rose-Marie. *Ted Trindell, Metis Witness to the North.* Vancouver: Tillacum Library, 1986.

National Geographic Society. *America's Majestic Canyons.* Washington, D.C.: National Geographic Society, 1979.

Overvold, Joanne. *A Portrayal of Our Metis Heritage.* Yellowknife: The Metis Association of the Northwest Territories, 1976.

Patterson, R. M. *The Dangerous River.* London: George Allen and Unwin Ltd., 1954.

Porsild, A.E., and Cody, W.J. *Vascular Plants of Continental Northwest Territories, Canada.* Ottawa: National Museums of Natural Sciences, 1980.

Scotter, G.W., Carbyn, N.L., Neily, W.P., Henry, J.D. *Birds of Nahanni National Park, Northwest Territories.* Regina: Saskatchewan Natural History Society, 1985.

Scotter, G.W., and Henry, J.D. *Vegetation, Wildlife and Recreational Assessment of Deadmen Valley, Nahanni National Park.* Edmonton: Canadian Wildlife Service, 1978.

Sturtevant, William C., and Helm, June, eds. *Handbook of North American Indians: Subarctic, Vol.6.* Washington: Smithsonian Institution, 1981.

Tetso, John. *Trapping is My Life.* Toronto: Peter Martin Associates Limited, 1970.

Thom, Margaret M., and Blondin-Townsend, Ethel. *Nahecho Keh – Our Elders.* Fort Providence: Slavey Research Project, 1987.

Thorpe, William E. *Assessment of Potential Spelunking Opportunities for the Visiting Public in Nahanni National Park Reserve.* Ottawa: Environment Canada – Parks, 1983.

Turner, Dick. *Nahanni.* Surrey: Hancock House Publishers Ltd., 1975.

Turner, Dick. *Wings of the North.* Surrey: Hancock House Publishers Ltd., 1980.

Walker, Marilyn. *Harvesting the Northern Wild.* Yellowknife: Outcrop Ltd., 1984.

White, Wendell E. *Nahanni Oral History, Nahanni National Park Area.* Ottawa: Environment Canada – Parks, 1987.

White, Wendell E. *The Birth of Nahanni "Nahande Beguli": A Local History of the People of Nahanni Butte.* Nahanni Butte: Unpublished, 1984.

*For those interested in a detailed and highly readable history of the area, we strongly recommend the Master's thesis written by Kerry Abel.

**The excellent reports of Professor Derek Ford of McMaster University, Department of Geography, Hamilton, Ontario, are extremely well-written and highly informative. We encourage anyone interested in this area's geology to inquire about these documents, which are available on loan from Environment Canada – Parks, Documentation Centre, Hull, Quebec.

PLATE 110 *Northern Blue Butterfly and Dried Grasses — July 1987*

PLANNING & LOGISTICS	Pat & Rosemarie Keough, Nahanni Productions Inc. Jim Broadbent, Okanagan Helicopters Ltd. Linda Davis, Canadian Airlines International Ltd. Derek Ford, McMaster University, Geography Department Ted Grant, Simpson Air (1981) Ltd. Ruth Montgomery, Canadian Airlines International Ltd. John Sheehan, Government of the Northwest Territories Nick Sibbeston, Government of the Northwest Territories
DESIGN	Pat & Rosemarie Keough, Nahanni Productions Inc.
TYPOGRAPHY & ASSEMBLY	Brant Cowie, ArtPlus Ltd. Heather Clark, Donna Guilfoyle, Ruth Nicholson, Paul Payer, Lorraine Smith, Cathy Campion, ArtPlus Ltd.
TYPE OUTPUT	Tony Gordon Limited
PRODUCTION	Pat & Rosemarie Keough, Nahanni Productions Inc. Mike Wallace, Stoddart Publishing Co. Limited
EDITORIAL	Heather Lang-Runtz
CARTOGRAPHY	William Constable
HISTORICAL PHOTO RESTORATION	Glynis Doorbar, Photospot Bryan Evans
COLOUR SEPARATION, PRINTING & BINDING	Dai Nippon Printing Company Limited

A STODDART / NAHANNI PRODUCTION